T0220317

Building a 2D Game Physics Engine

Using HTML5 and JavaScript

Michael Tanaya

Huaming Chen

Jebediah Pavleas

Kelvin Sung

Apress®

Building a 2D Game Physics Engine: Using HTML5 and JavaScript

Michael Tanaya
Bothell, Washington, USA

Huaming Chen
Bothell, Washington, USA

Jebediah Pavleas
Kenmore, Washington, USA

Kelvin Sung
Woodinville, Washington, USA

ISBN-13 (pbk): 978-1-4842-2582-0
DOI 10.1007/978-1-4842-2583-7

ISBN-13 (electronic): 978-1-4842-2583-7

Library of Congress Control Number: 2017930129

Cover image designed by Freepik

Managing Director: Welmoed Spahr
Lead Editor: Steve Anglin
Development Editor: Matthew Moodie
Technical Reviewer: Jason Sturges
Coordinating Editor: Mark Powers
Copy Editor: Larissa Shmailo
Compositor: SPi Global
Indexer: SPi Global
Artist: SPi Global

Distributed to the book trade worldwide by Springer Science+Business Media New York, 233 Spring Street, 6th Floor, New York, NY 10013. Phone 1-800-SPRINGER, fax (201) 348-4505, e-mail orders-ny@springer-sbm.com, or visit www.springeronline.com. Apress Media, LLC is a California LLC and the sole member (owner) is Springer Science + Business Media Finance Inc (SSBM Finance Inc). SSBM Finance Inc is a **Delaware** corporation.

For information on translations, please e-mail rights@apress.com, or visit http://www.apress.com/us/services/rights-permission.

Apress titles may be purchased in bulk for academic, corporate, or promotional use. eBook versions and licenses are also available for most titles. For more information, reference our Print and eBook Bulk Sales web page at http://www.apress.com/us/services/bulk-sales.

Any source code or other supplementary material referenced by the author in this book is available to readers for download via the book's product page, located at www.apress.com/9781484225820. For more detailed information, please visit http://www.apress.com/us/services/source-code.

Printed on acid-free paper

To my love, Josephine Janice, for her companionship through many long nights of writing, and my parents, Hendi and Ros, for their support, advice, and love.

—Michael Tanaya

To my parents, Chen Yaoqing and Tang Hua, for their encouragements and love.

—Huaming Chen

To my Mother, Diana, for the love and support she has given me throughout my life.

—Jebediah Pavleas

To my wife, Clover, and our girls, Jean and Ruth, for completing my life

—Kelvin Sung

Contents at a Glance

Contents

About the Authors

Michael Tanaya is an international graduate student from Indonesia in the Computer Science and Software Engineering program at the University of Washington Bothell (UWB). He received his Bachelor of Computer Science in 2014 from the University of Minnesota at Twin Cities. During his time as an undergraduate, he took interests in computer games and web application development. In his free time, he enjoys playing competitive video games, designing and developing video games with Unity™ and Cocos2D™. Currently Michael is working with Professor Kelvin Sung on developing a system that integrates Virtual and Augmented Reality technologies in creating a learning multimedia environment for active hands-on learning. He will be graduating in Spring 2017.

Huaming Chen is an international graduate student from China in the Computer Science and Software Engineering program at the University of Washington Bothell (UWB). He received dual undergraduate degrees, in Computer Science and Economics, from Xiamen University in 2015. During his time as an undergraduate, he was interested in data mining and videogame design. His project includes a structure of website groups that related to each other and a software system that recommends useful information based on the website groups. He also developed a mobile game based on Unity3D. Currently, Huaming is working on a project that focuses on designing videogames that simplify vision therapy for children. He will be graduating in Spring 2017.

Jebediah Pavleas is a software engineer who received his Master of Science in Computer Science and Software Engineering from the University of Washington Bothell (UWB) in 2016 as well as a Bachelor of Science in 2012, where he was the recipient of the Chancellor's Medal for his class. In 2015 he interned at Microsoft Research, where he worked on improving the safety and usability of an eye gaze wheelchair. During his time as a student, he took a great interest in both computer graphics and games. His projects included an interactive math application that utilizes Microsoft's Kinect sensor to teach algebra and a 2D role-playing game designed to teach students introductory programming concepts. Relating to these projects, he co-authored publications in *IEEE Computers* and *The Journal of Computing Sciences in Colleges*. He enjoys designing, building, and playing games of all kinds, as well as adapting technology for improved accessibility. Jebediah is also the primary author of *Learn 2D Game Development with C#* (APress, December 2013) and co-author of *Build Your Own 2D Game Engine and Create Great Web Games* (Apress, October 2015).

Kelvin Sung is a professor with the Computing and Software Systems division at University of Washington Bothell (UWB). He received his Ph.D. in Computer Science from the University of Illinois at Urbana-Champaign. Kelvin's background is in computer graphics, hardware, and machine architecture. He came to UWB from Alias|Wavefront (now part of Autodesk), where he played a key role in designing and implementing the Maya Renderer, an Academy Award-winning image generation system. Funded by Microsoft Research and the National Science Foundation, Kelvin's recent work focused on the intersection of video game mechanics, solutions to real-world problems, and mobile technologies. Together with his students, Kelvin has co-authored three recent books: one in computer graphics (*Essentials of Interactive Computer Graphics: Concepts and Implementations*, A.K. Peters, 2008), and the others in 2D game engines (*Learn 2D Game Development with C#*, APress, December 2013; and *Build Your Own 2D Game Engine and Create Great Web Games*, Apress, October 2015).

About the Technical Reviewer

Jason Sturges is a cutting edge technologist focused on ubiquitous delivery of immersive user experiences. Coming from a visualization background, he's always pushing the boundaries of computer graphics to the widest reach across platforms while maintaining natural and intuitive usability per device. From interactivity, motion, and animation to creative design, he has worked with numerous creative agencies on projects from kiosks to video walls to Microsoft Kinect games. Most recently, the core of his work has been mobile apps. Committed to the open source community, he is also a frequent contributor at GitHub and Stack Overflow as a community resource leveraging modern standards, solid design patterns, and best practices in multiple developer tool chains for web, mobile, desktop, and beyond.

Acknowledgments

This and our prior books on Games and Game Engine development are the direct result of the authors learning from building games for the Game-Themed CS1/2: Empowering the Faculty project, funded by the Transforming Undergraduate Education in Science Technology, Engineering, and Mathematics (TUES) Program, National Science Foundation (NSF) (award number DUE-1140410). We would like to thank NSF officers Suzanne Westbrook for believing in our project and Jane Prey, Valerie Bar, and Paul Tymann for their encouragement.

The invaluable collaboration between the technical team in the Game-Themed Research Group (https://depts.washington.edu/cmmr/GTCS/) and the design team in the Digital Future Lab (http://www.bothell.washington.edu/digitalfuture) at the University of Washington Bothell (where much of our learning occurred during the production of the many casual games for teaching introductory programming concepts) formed the foundation that allowed the development of this book. Thank you to all the participants of this research undertaking. The authors would also like to thank the students at the University of Washington Bothell for the games they built from the course CSS385: Introduction to Game Development (see http://courses.washington.edu/css385). Their interest and passion for games has provided us with the ideal deployment vehicle and are a source of continuous inspiration. They have tested, retested, contributed to, and assisted in the formation and organization of the contents of this book.

Jebediah Pavleas would like to thank the Computing and Software Systems Division at the University of Washington Bothell for the generous tuition scholarships that funded his education throughout his participation with this book project.

Thanks to Clover Wai, for once again helping us with the figures and illustrations in this book.

We also want to thank Steve Anglin at Apress for believing in this project, to our editor Mark Powers for his patience and toleration with our constantly behind-schedule frenzy. Finally, we would like to thank Jason Sturges for his insightful technical feedback.

All opinions, findings, conclusions, and recommendations in this work are those of the authors and do not necessarily reflect the views of the sponsors.

Introduction

Welcome to *Building a 2D Game Physics Engine: Using HTML5 and JavaScript*. Because you have picked up this book, you are likely interested in the details of a game physics engine and the creation of your own games to be played over the Internet. This book teaches you how to build a 2D game physics engine by covering the involved technical concepts, and providing detailed implementations for you to follow. The source code in this book is provided in HTML5 and JavaScript, which are technologies that are freely available and supported by virtually all web browsers. After reading this book, the game physics engine you develop will be playable through a web browser from anywhere on the Internet.

This book focuses only on the relevant concepts and implementation details for building a 2D game physics engine. The presentations are tightly integrated with the analysis and development of source code. Much of the book guides you in implementing related concepts and building blocks while the actual functioning engine only becomes available towards the end. Some of the algorithms and mathematics can be challenging. Be patient. It will all pay off by the end of Chapter 4. By Chapter 5, you will be familiar with the concepts and technical details of 2D game physics engines, and feel competent in implementing the associated functionality.

Who Should Read This Book

This book is targeted toward programmers who are familiar with basic object-oriented programming concepts and have a basic to intermediate knowledge of an object-oriented programming language such as Java or C#. For example, if you are a student who has taken a few introductory programming courses, an experienced developer who is new to games and graphics programming, or a self-taught programming enthusiast, you will be able to follow the concepts and code presented in this book with little trouble. If you're new to programming in general, it is suggested that you first become comfortable with the JavaScript programming language and concepts in object-oriented programming before tackling the content provided in this book.

Assumptions

You should have some basic background in Newtonian Mechanics and be experienced with programming in an object-oriented programming language, such as Java or C#. Knowledge and expertise in JavaScript would be a plus but is not necessary. The examples in this book were created with the assumption that you understand data encapsulation and inheritance. In addition, you should be familiar with basic data structures such as linked lists and dictionaries, and be comfortable working with the fundamentals of algebra and geometry, particularly linear equations and coordinate systems.

Who Should Not Read This Book

This book is not designed to teach readers how to program, the formal mathematics of physics, nor does it attempt to explain the intricate details of HTML5 or JavaScript. If you have no prior experience developing software with an object-oriented programming language, you will probably find the examples in this book difficult to follow.

On the other hand, if you have an extensive background in game physics engine development based on other platforms, the content in this book will be too basic; this is a book intended for developers without 2D game physics engine development experience.

Organization of This Book

This book teaches how to develop a game physics engine by describing the foundational infrastructure, collision detection algorithms, information that should be gathered during a collision, and approaches to resolving and computing responses after a collision.

Chapter 2 introduces the foundational infrastructure, including the mathematics library, and supporting framework for game loop, user input, and basic drawing. Chapter 3 focuses on how to detect collisions covering efficiency, generality, and vital information to record during a collision. Chapter 4 integrates the building blocks from the previous two chapters and presents the details on simulating motions and computing responses after a collision. Chapter 5 summarizes the book with a demonstration program and references for further readings.

Code Samples

Every chapter in this book includes examples that let you interactively experiment with and learn the new materials. You can download the source code for all the projects, including the associated assets (images, audio clips, or fonts), from the following page: www.apress.com/9781484225820.

Follow the instructions to download the 9781484225820.zip file. To install the code samples, unzip the 9781484225820.zip file. You should see a folder structure that is organized by chapter numbers. Within each folder are subfolders containing NetBeans projects that correspond to sections of this book.

CHAPTER 1

■ ■ ■

Introduction to 2D Game Physics Engine Development

Physics engines play an important part in many types of games. A believable physics interaction between game objects has become a key element of most modern PC and console games as well as, more recently, browser and smartphone games. The range of topics within physics for games is broad and includes, but is not limited to, areas such as rigid body, fluid dynamics, soft-body, vehicle physics, and particle physics. This book will cover the fundamental topics needed for you to get started in understanding and building a general purpose, rigid body physics engine in two dimensions. The book also aims to provide you with a reusable game physics engine, which can be used for your own games, by guiding you through the process of building a physics engine step-by-step from scratch. This way you will gain a foundational understanding of the concepts and components required for a typical 2D rigid body system.

While you can just download a physics engine library and continue on with your game or engine development, building your own game engine from scratch has its own advantages. Besides giving you an underlying understanding of how the physics engine operates, it gives you more control over the flexibility, performance, functionality, and usability of the engine itself.

As stated, this book will cover the foundation of 2D rigid body physics. The topics will include properties and behavior of rigid bodies, collision detection, collision information encoding, and collision response. The goal is to obtain a fundamental understanding of these concepts which are required to build a usable physics engine.

The book approaches physics engine development from three important avenues: practicality, approachability, and reusability. While reading the book, we want you to get involved and experience the process of building the game engine. The step-by-step guide should facilitate the practicality of this book. The theories and practices introduced in this book are based on research and investigation from many sources which cover the topics in varying detail. The information is presented in a way that is approachable, by allowing you to follow along as each code snippet is explained in parallel to the overall concepts behind

---

Electronic supplementary material The online version of this chapter (doi:10.1007/978-1-4842-2583-7_1) contains supplementary material, which is available to authorized users.

© Michael Tanaya, Huaming Chen, Jebediah Pavleas and Kelvin Sung 2017
M. Tanaya et al., *Building a 2D Game Physics Engine*, DOI 10.1007/978-1-4842-2583-7_1

each component of the engine. After following along and creating your own engine, you will be able to extend and reuse the finished product by adding your own features.

This chapter describes the implementation technology and organization of the book. The discussion then leads you through the steps of downloading, installing, and setting up the development environment; guides you through building your first HTML5 application; and extends this first application with the JavaScript programming language to run your first simulation.

Setting Up Your Development Environment

The physics engine you are going to build will be accessible through web browsers that could be running on any operating system (OS). The development environment you are about to set up is also OS agnostic. For simplicity, the following instructions are based on a Windows 7/8/10 OS. You should be able to reproduce a similar environment with minor modifications in a Unix-based environment like the Apple macOS or Ubuntu.

Your development process includes an integrated development environment (IDE) and a runtime web browser that is capable of hosting the running game engine. The most convenient systems we have found are the NetBeans IDE with the Google Chrome web browser as the runtime environment. Here are the details:

- *IDE*: All projects in this book are based on the NetBeans IDE. You can download and install the bundle for HTML5 and PHP from https://netbeans.org/downloads.

- *Runtime environment*: You will execute your projects in the Google Chrome web browser. You can download and install this browser from https://www.google.com/chrome/browser/.

- *Connector Google Chrome plug-in*: This is a Google Chrome extension that connects the web browser to the NetBeans IDE to support HTML5 development. You can download and install this extension from https://chrome.google.com/webstore/detail/netbeans-connector/hafdlehgocfcodbgjnpecfajgkeejnaa. The download will automatically install the plug-in to Google Chrome. You may have to restart your computer to complete the installation.

Notice that there are no specific system requirements to support the JavaScript programming language or HTML5. All these technologies are embedded in the web browser runtime environment.

■ **Note** As mentioned, we chose a NetBeans-based development environment because we found it to be the most convenient. There are many other alternatives that are also free, including and not limited to IntelliJ IDEA, Eclipse, Sublime, Microsoft's Visual Studio Code, and Adobe Brackets.

Downloading and Installing JavaScript Syntax Checker

We have found JSLint to be an effective tool in detecting potential JavaScript source code errors. You can download and install JSLint as a plug-in to the NetBeans IDE with the following steps:

- Download it from http://plugins.netbeans.org/ plugin/40893/jslint. Make sure to take note of the location of the downloaded file.

- Start NetBeans, select Tools ➤ Plugins, and go to the Downloaded tab.

- Click the Add Plugins button and search for the downloaded file from step 1. Double-click this file to install the plug-in.

The following are some useful references for working with JSLint:

- For instructions on how to work with JSLint, see http://www.jslint.com/help.html.

- For details on how JSLint works, see http://plugins.netbeans.org/plugin/40893/jslint

Working in the NetBeans Development Environment

The NetBeans IDE is easy to work with, and the projects in this book require only the editor and debugger. To open a project, select File ➤ Open Projects. Once a project is open, you need to become familiarized with three basic windows, as illustrated in Figure 1-1.

- *Projects window*: This window displays the source code files of the project.

- *Editor window*: This window displays and allows you to edit the source code of your project. You can select the source code file to work with by double-clicking the corresponding file name in the Projects window.

- *Action Items window*: This window displays the error message output from the JSLint checker.

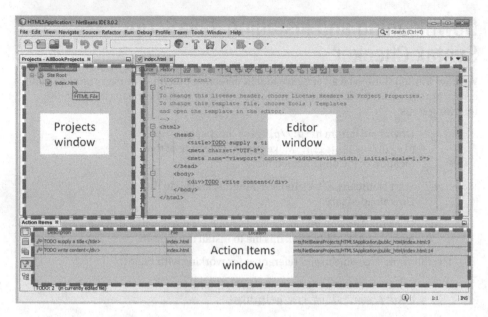

Figure 1-1. *The NetBeans IDE*

■ **Note** If you cannot see a window in the IDE, you can click the Window menu and select the name of the missing window to cause it to appear. For example, if you cannot see the Projects window in the IDE, you can select Window ➤ Projects to open it.

Creating an HTML5 Project in NetBeans

You are now ready to create your first HTML5 project.

1. Start NetBeans. Select File ➤ New Project (or press Ctrl+Shift+N), as shown in Figure 1-2. A New Project window will appear.

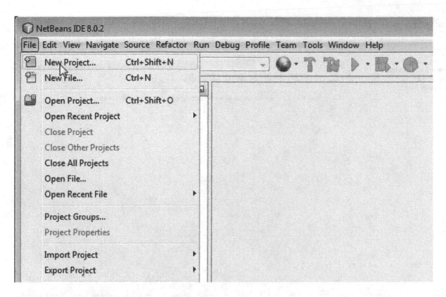

Figure 1-2. *Creating a new project*

2. In the New Project window, select HTML5 in the Categories section, and select HTML5 Application from the Projects section, as shown in Figure 1-3. Click the Next button to bring up the project configuration window.

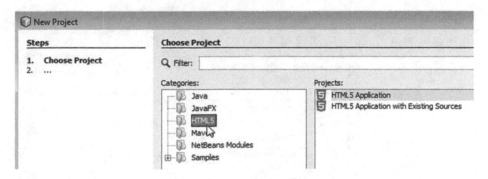

Figure 1-3. *Selecting the HTML5 project*

3. As shown in Figure 1-4, enter the name and location of the project, and click the Finish button to create your first HTML5 project.

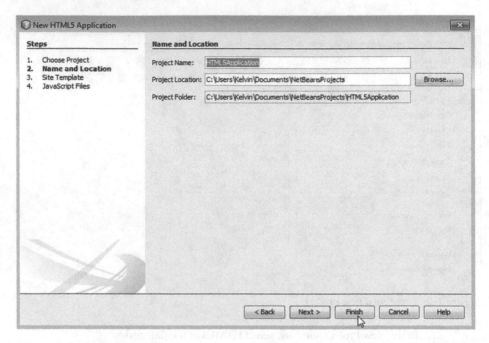

Figure 1-4. *Naming the project*

NetBeans will generate the template of a simple and complete HTML5 application project for you. Your IDE should look similar to Figure 1-5.

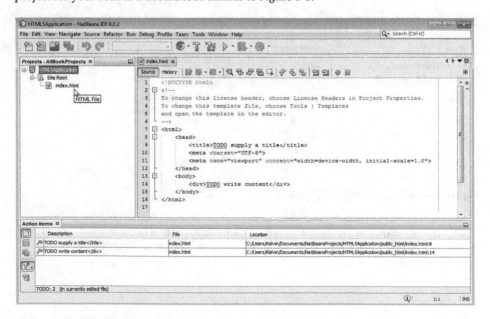

Figure 1-5. *The HTML5 application project*

By selecting and double-clicking the index.html file in the Projects window, you can open it in the Editor window and observe the content of the file. The contents are as follows:

```
<!DOCTYPE html>
<!--
To change this license header, choose License Headers in Project Properties.
To change this template file, choose Tools | Templates
and open the template in the editor.
-->
<html>
    <head>
        <title>TODO supply a title</title>
    </head>
    <body>
        <div>TODO write content</div>
    </body>
</html>
```

The first line declares the file to be an HTML file. The block that follows within the <!-- and --> tags is a comment block. The complementary <html></html> tags contain all the HTML code. In this case, the template defines the head and body sections. The head sets the title of the web page, and the body is where all the content for the web page will be located.

You can run this project by selecting Run ➤ Run Project or by pressing the F6 key. Figure 1-6 shows an example of what the default project looks like when you run it.

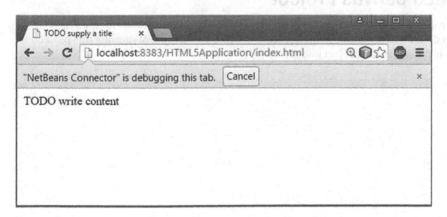

Figure 1-6. *Running the simple HTML5 project*

To stop the program, either close the web page or click the Cancel button in the browser to stop NetBeans from tracking the web page. You have successfully run your first HTML5 project. You can use this project to understand the IDE environment.

The Relationship Between the Project Files and the File System

Navigate to the HTML5Application project location on your file system, for example with the Explorer OS utility in Windows. You can observe that in the project folder, NetBeans has generated the nbProject, public_html, and test folders. Table 1-1 summarizes the purpose of these folders and the index.html file.

Table 1-1. *Folders and files in a NetBeans HTML5 project*

NetBeans HTML5 project: folder/file	Purpose
nbProject/	This folder contains the IDE configuration files. You will not modify any of the files in this folder.
public_html/	This is the root folder of your project. Source code and assets from your project will be created in this folder.
public_html/index.html	This is the default entry point for your web site. This file will be modified to load JavaScript source code files.
test/	This is the default folder for unit testing source code files. This folder is not used in this book and has been removed from all the projects.

HTML5 Canvas Project

This project demonstrates how to set up the core drawing functionality for the engine as well as define a user control script. Figure 1-7 shows an example of running this project, which is defined in the project folder.

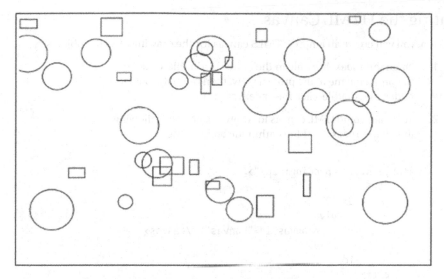

Figure 1-7. *Running the HTML5 project with drawing core and user control*

The goals of the project are as follows:

- To learn how to set up the HTML canvas element

- To learn how to retrieve the canvas element from an HTML document for use in JavaScript

- To learn how to create a reference context to an HTML canvas, and use it to manipulate the canvas

- To get familiar with basic user control scripting

Drawing Core

This engine will use simple drawing code for the sole purpose of simulating the physics engine code. After all, the only thing the simulation needs to show is how simple objects interact after the physics engine code is implemented. Thus, advanced graphical functionalities such as illumination, texturing, or shadow rendering will only serve to further complicate the code base. For that reason, a simple HTML5 canvas with primitive drawing support will serve the purpose of rendering the physics simulation during creation and debugging.

Creating the HTML Canvas

In this step, you will create an empty HTML5 canvas for the drawing of all the objects.

1. Open the index.html file in the editor by double-clicking the project name in the project view, then open the Site Root folder, and double-click the index.html file.

2. To create your HTML canvas for drawing, add the following line in the index.html file within the body element

```
<table style="padding: 2px">
    <tr>
        <td>
            <div>
                <canvas id="canvas"></canvas>
            </div>
        </td>
    </tr>
</table>
```

The code defines a canvas element with an id of canvas. An id is the name of the element and can be used to retrieve the corresponding element when the web page is loaded. Notice that no width and height is specified in the code. This is because you will specify those attributes in the next step. You will use the canvas id to retrieve the reference to the actual canvas drawing area where you will draw into.

Creating the Core Script

This section details the steps needed to create your first script, the drawing canvas initialization. This script will evolve to contain more core functionalities for the physics engine. For this step, you will only write the initialization code for the drawing canvas.

1. Create a new folder named EngineCore inside the SiteRoot (or public_html) folder by right-clicking and creating a new folder.

2. Create a new JavaScript file within the EngineCore folder by right-clicking the EngineCore folder. Name the file Core.js.

3. Open the new Core.js file for editing.

4. Create a static reference to gEngine by adding the following code.

```
var gEngine = gEngine || {};
gEngine.Core = (function () {
}());
```

gEngine.Core is where all the physics engine core functionality will reside.

■ **Note** All global variable names begin with a "g" and are followed by a capital letter, as in gEngine.

5. Inside the gEngine.Core you want to access and define the width and height of the canvas element. To do this you will create a variable mCanvas, and reference it to the canvas element of index.html such that you could set and modify the canvas attributes. You also need the variable mContext, which will keep a reference to all the methods and properties needed to draw into the canvas. Add the following code to accomplish these.

```
var mCanvas, mContext, mWidth = 800, mHeight = 450;
mCanvas = document.getElementById('canvas');
mContext = mCanvas.getContext('2d');
mCanvas.height = mHeight;
mCanvas.width = mWidth;
```

■ **Note** All instance variable names begin with an "m" and are followed by a capital letter, as in mCanvas.

6. Create an object variable mPublic, because you need to make some of the engine core variables and functions accessible by other scripts later in the development of the engine. For now, mPublic will only need to keep three variables accessible, that is, the width and height of canvas, and the mContext to draw into the canvas.

```
var mPublic = {
    mWidth: mWidth,
    mHeight: mHeight,
    mContext: mContext
};
return mPublic;
```

7. Finally, for the Core.js to be included in the simulation, you need to add it into the index.html file. To do this, simply add the following code inside the body element.

```
<script type="text/javascript" src="EngineCore/Core.js"></script>
```

User Control

In this section, you will be introduced to basic user control event handlers using JavaScript. This is to enable you to test your implementation in every step of the physics engine's incremental development. For this chapter, the user control script will be used to test if you have correctly initialized the canvas and implemented drawing functionality properly.

Creating User Control Script

Let's get started:

1. Create a new JavaScript File within the SiteRoot folder by right-clicking the SiteRoot (or public_html) folder. Name the file UserControl.js.

2. Open the new UserControl.js file for editing

3. Here you want to create a function that will handle all the keyboard input. Let's name the function userControl. This function will have a variable called keycode that will keep track of the user keyboard input. To do this, add the following code inside the UserControl.js.

    ```
    function userControl(event) {
        var keycode;
    }
    ```

4. Since some browsers handle input events differently, you want to know in which type of browser the simulation will run. Add the following code within the control function to distinguish between an IE key event handler and other browser key event handler.

    ```
    if (window.event) { // IE
        keycode = event.keyCode;
    }
    else if (event.which) { // Netscape/Firefox/Opera
        keycode = event.which;
    }
    ```

This script will enable you to handle keyboard input events from the browser as well as process the input and response accordingly. In this case, you want to test the canvas you just created in the last section. This testing can be achieved by drawing rectangles and circles when keyboard inputs are received, as detailed in the next section.

Using the User Control Script

In this section, you will complete the UserControl.js file for this chapter by adding some user input responses to draw a rectangle or a circle in random positions on the canvas when F or G keys are pressed.

The control script will be triggered by the HTML onkeydown event. It is important to recognize that in the browser, each keyboard key is associated with a unique key code. For example, "a" is associated with a keycode of 65, "b" is 66, and so on.

■ **Note** The UserControl.js will evolve over the development to handle more keyboard inputs and more complex responses.

---

1. Open the UserControl.js file for edit.

2. You need to access the width and height of canvas, and the context to draw into the canvas. Add the following lines of code inside the control function.

```
var width = gEngine.Core.mWidth;
var height = gEngine.Core.mHeight;
var context = gEngine.Core.mContext;
```

3. Create a rectangle at a random position if the "F" key (with key code value of 70) is pressed, and a circle if the "G" key (with key code value of 71) is pressed. Add the following lines to accomplish this task.

```
if (keycode === 70) { //f
    //create new Rectangle at random position
    context.strokeRect(Math.random() * width * 0.8,
    // x position of center
    Math.random() * height * 0.8,
    // y position of center
    Math.random() * 30 + 10, Math.random() * 30 + 10);
    // width and height location
}
if (keycode === 71) { //g
    //create new Circle at random position
    context.beginPath();
    //draw a circle
    context.arc(Math.random() * width * 0.8,
    // x position of center
    Math.random() * height * 0.8,
    // y position of center
    Math.random() * 30 + 10, 0, Math.PI * 2, true);
```

```
        // radius
        context.closePath();
        context.stroke();
}
```

4. Next, for the UserControl.js to be included in the simulation,
    you need to add it into the index.html file. To do this, simply
    add the following code inside the body element.

```
<script type="text/javascript" src="EngineCore/Control.js">
</script>
```

5. Finally, you want HTML to handle the key pressing event.
    Open the index.html file to edit and add the onkeydown
    attribute to the body tag to call your JavaScript function
    control. Modify your index.html file so the body tag will look
    like the following.

```
<body onkeydown="return userControl(event);" >
```

Now if you run the project and press the key F or G, the simulation will draw either
a circle or rectangle at a random position with random sizes as shown in Figure 1-7 above.

Summary

By this point the physics engine's basic drawing function has been initialized, and
should be able to draw a rectangle and a circle onto the canvas with basic input required
from the user. In this chapter, you have structured the source code that supports future
increase in complexity with a simple way to draw rigid bodies. You are now ready to
extend the functionalities and features of your project into a physics engine. The next
chapter will focus on the core functionalities needed for any game or physics engine
(engine loops, vector calculation), as well as evolving rectangles and circles into rigid
body object-oriented objects to encapsulate their drawing and behaviors.

CHAPTER 2

■ ■ ■

Implementing the 2D Physics Engine Core

In the previous chapter, you implemented functionality to support basic drawing operations. Drawing is the first step to constructing your physics engine because it allows you to observe the output while continuing to expand the engine's capabilities. In this chapter, two critical components for 2D physics simulations, the core engine loop and rigid shape class, will be examined and added to the engine. The core engine loop, or the engine loop, allows the engine to control and handle the real-time interaction of game objects, while the rigid shape class abstracts and hides the detailed information such as positions and rotation angles that are required for future physics calculations.

This chapter begins with the brief coverage of a simple vector calculation library. It is assumed that you have a background in basic vector operations in 2D space, and thus the required code is provided without extensive conceptual explanations. The chapter then introduces you to a rigid shape class, a critical abstraction that will encapsulate all the information of an object that is required in a physics simulation, for example (as will be introduced in a following chapter) information such as width, height, center position, mass, inertia, and friction. This information presented through the rigid shape class will be utilized throughout the engine's evolution into a fully featured 2D game physics library. For this chapter you will begin with the creation of the rigid shape class that only contains information for drawing of the object onto the canvas. Lastly, you will be introduced to one of the more important components of the physics engine, the core engine loop.

After completing this chapter, you will be able to:

- Control the position and rotation of objects based on user keyboard input.

- Simulate gravity that affects all objects in the scene and the ability to toggle gravity on and off.

- Select and display the properties of a specific object.

- Reset the scene.

© Michael Tanaya, Huaming Chen, Jebediah Pavleas and Kelvin Sung 2017   15
M. Tanaya et al., *Building a 2D Game Physics Engine*, DOI 10.1007/978-1-4842-2583-7_2

Vector Calculation Library

Physics simulation requires a vector library to represent object positions and orientations, and to support the computations involved in the simulation that changes these quantities. The computation involved in 2D physics simulations are basic vector operations, including addition, subtraction, scaling, cross product, etc. For this reason, you will create a simple Vec2 vector math library to be included in all subsequent projects.

Creating the Library

In this step, you will create a new file within a new Library folder to support all the required calculations.

1. Create a new folder name Lib inside the SiteRoot (or public_ html) folder by right-clicking and creating a new folder.

2. Create a new JavaScript file within the Library folder by right-clicking the Lib folder. Name the file Vec2.js.

3. Open the new Vec2.js file for editing.

4. Add the Vec2 constructor.

    ```
    var Vec2 = function (x, y) {
        this.x = x;
        this.y = y;
    };
    ```

5. Add all the functions to support basic vector operations.

    ```
    Vec2.prototype.length = function () {
        return Math.sqrt(this.x * this.x + this.y * this.y);
    };

    Vec2.prototype.add = function (vec) {
        return new Vec2(vec.x + this.x, vec.y + this.y);
    };

    Vec2.prototype.subtract = function (vec) {
        return new Vec2(this.x - vec.x, this.y - vec.y);
    };

    Vec2.prototype.scale = function (n) {
        return new Vec2(this.x * n, this.y * n);
    };
    ```

```javascript
Vec2.prototype.dot = function (vec) {
    return (this.x * vec.x + this.y * vec.y);
};

Vec2.prototype.cross = function (vec) {
    return (this.x * vec.y - this.y * vec.x);
};

Vec2.prototype.rotate = function (center, angle) {
    //rotate in counterclockwise
    var r = [];
    var x = this.x - center.x;
    var y = this.y - center.y;
    r[0] = x * Math.cos(angle) - y * Math.sin(angle);
    r[1] = x * Math.sin(angle) + y * Math.cos(angle);
    r[0] += center.x;
    r[1] += center.y;
    return new Vec2(r[0], r[1]);
};

Vec2.prototype.normalize = function () {
    var len = this.length();
    if (len > 0) {
        len = 1 / len;
    }
    return new Vec2(this.x * len, this.y * len);
};

Vec2.prototype.distance = function (vec) {
    var x = this.x - vec.x;
    var y = this.y - vec.y;
    return Math.sqrt(x * x + y * y);
};
```

With these functions defined, it is now possible to operate on vectors to calculate and manipulate the position, size, and orientation of objects drawn on the canvas. It is expected that you understand these elementary operators. Do not forget to include the new library in the project by adding the new file into the index.html using the <script> tag, like so:

```html
<script type="text/javascript" src="Lib/Vec2.js"></script>
```

Physics Engine and Rigid Shapes

This book focuses on primitive objects that do not change shape during their physical interactions, or objects that are rigid. For example, a falling Lego block bouncing off of your desk and landing on a hardwood floor would be considered an interaction between rigid objects. This type of simulation is known as a rigid body physics simulation, or more simply a rigid body simulation.

The computation involved in simulating the interactions between arbitrary rigid shapes can be algorithmically complicated and computationally costly. For these reasons, rigid body simulations are often based on a limited set of simple geometric shapes, for example, rigid circles and rectangles. In typical game engines, these simple rigid shapes can be *attached* to geometrically complex game objects for approximating their physics simulations, for example, attaching rigid circles on spaceships and using the rigid body physics simulation of the rigid circles to approximate the physical interactions between the spaceships.

The physics engine you will build is based on simulating the interactions between rigid circles and rectangles. This simulation consists of four fundamental steps:

1. Implementing motions

2. Detecting collisions

3. Resolving the collisions

4. Deriving responses to the collisions

The rest of this chapter leads you to build the infrastructure to represent simple rigid circles and rectangles. The following chapters present the intricate details of collision detection, motion approximation, collision resolution, and collision responses.

The Rigid Shape Project

This project demonstrates how to implement the basic infrastructure to encapsulate the characteristics of a rigid body. You can see an example of this project running in Figure 2-1.

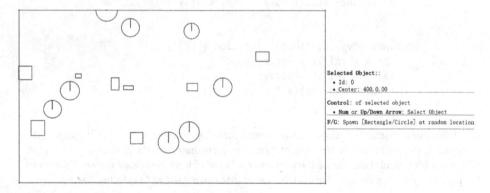

Figure 2-1. Running the Rigid Shape Project

The source code to this project is defined in the Rigid Shape Project folder. Project Goals:

- To define the base class for all rigid shape objects.

- To lay the foundation for building a rigid shape physics simulator.

- To understand the relationships between rigid shape classes and the engine core functionality.

- To define an initial scene for testing your implement.

The List Object in Engine Core

You will begin by defining a list object, mAllObjects, to keep track of all defined rigid shapes. As you will see in the next chapter, the mAllObjects list allows the simulation of physical interaction among all defined rigid shapes. To conveniently support the simulation computation, the mAllObjects list is defined in the gEngine.Core component.

1. Edit Core.js and add the following line inside gEngine.Core. This creates a list for keeping track of all defined rigid shapes.

```
var mAllObjects = [];
```

2. Update the mPublic variable in the Core.js to allow access to the newly defined list object. This is accomplished in the following code snippet.

```
var mPublic = {
    mAllObjects: mAllObjects,
    mWidth: mWidth,
    mHeight: mHeight,
    mContext: mContext
};
```

The Rigid Shape Base Class

You can now define a base class for the rectangle and circle shape objects. This base class will encapsulate all the functionality that is common to the two shapes.

1. Start by creating a new subfolder called RigidBody under the SiteRoot (or public_html) folder. In the RigidBody folder, create a new file and name it RigidShape.js

2. Edit RigidShape.js to define the constructor. For now the constructor only receives one vector argument representing the center of the object. The rotation angle of the rigid shape has a default value of 0. The created object is then pushed into the global object list, mAllObjects.

```
function RigidShape(center) {
    this.mCenter = center;
    this.mAngle = 0;
    gEngine.Core.mAllObjects.push(this);
}
```

The Rigid Rectangle Class

With the base abstract class for rigid shapes defined, you can now create the first concrete rigid shape, the rigid rectangle.

1. Under the RigidBody folder, create a new file and name it Rectangle.js.

2. Edit this file to create a constructor that receives the center, a width and height properties. In the constructor, define the type of rigid body as Rectangle, allocate an array to store the vertex positions of the rectangle, and a separate array to store the face normal vectors (to be discussed later).

```
var Rectangle = function (center, width, height) {
    RigidShape.call(this, center);
    this.mType = "Rectangle";
    this.mWidth = width;
    this.mHeight = height;
    this.mVertex = [];
    this.mFaceNormal = [];
};
```

3. In the constructor, compute the vertex positions of the rectangle using the center, width, and height information.

```
//0--TopLeft;1--TopRight;2--BottomRight;3--BottomLeft
this.mVertex[0] = new Vec2(center.x - width / 2, center.y -
height / 2);
this.mVertex[1] = new Vec2(center.x + width / 2, center.y -
height / 2);
this.mVertex[2] = new Vec2(center.x + width / 2, center.y +
height / 2);
this.mVertex[3] = new Vec2(center.x - width / 2, center.y +
height / 2);
```

4. Next, compute the face normal vectors. As illustrated in Figure 2-2, face normals are vectors that are perpendicular to the edges and point away from the center of the rectangle. Notice that the face normal vectors are normalized with a length of 1. In addition, notice the relationship between the rectangle vertices and the corresponding face normals. Face normal index-0 is in the same direction as the vector from vertex 2 to 1. This direction is perpendicular to the edge formed by vertices 0 and 1. In this way, face normal index-0 is the direction pointing away from the rectangle that is perpendicular to the first edge, and so on. The face normal vectors will be used later for determining collisions.

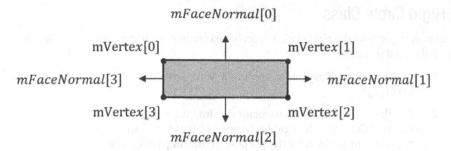

Figure 2-2. *The face normals of a rectangle*

```
//0--Top;1--Right;2--Bottom;3--Left
//mFaceNormal is normal of face toward outside of rectangle
this.mFaceNormal[0] = this.mVertex[1].subtract(this.mVertex[2]);
this.mFaceNormal[0] = this.mFaceNormal[0].normalize();
this.mFaceNormal[1] = this.mVertex[2].subtract(this.mVertex[3]);
this.mFaceNormal[1] = this.mFaceNormal[1].normalize();
this.mFaceNormal[2] = this.mVertex[3].subtract(this.mVertex[0]);
this.mFaceNormal[2] = this.mFaceNormal[2].normalize();
this.mFaceNormal[3] = this.mVertex[0].subtract(this.mVertex[1]);
this.mFaceNormal[3] = this.mFaceNormal[3].normalize();
```

5. Ensure the newly defined Rectangle class properly inherits
    from the RigidShape base class by including the following
    code after the constructor.

```
var prototype = Object.create(RigidShape.prototype);
prototype.constructor = Rectangle;
Rectangle.prototype = prototype;
```

6. Now you can create the draw function for the rectangle
    object. The strokeRect function of the context, a reference
    to the canvas, is invoked to accomplish this. Corresponding
    translation and rotation must be defined in order to draw
    the rectangle at the proper position and orientation. The
    implementation is shown as follows.

```
Rectangle.prototype.draw = function (context) {
    context.save();
    context.translate(this.mVertex[0].x, this.mVertex[0].y);
    context.rotate(this.mAngle);
    context.strokeRect(0, 0, this.mWidth, this.mHeight);
    context.restore();
};
```

The Rigid Circle Class

You can now implement the rigid circle object based on an overall structure that is similar to that of the rigid rectangle.

1. Under the RigidBody folder, create a new file and name it Circle.js.

2. Edit this file to create a constructor that initializes the radius of the circle, the rigid body type as Circle, and an mStartpoint position for the purpose of drawing a reference line to visualize the rotation angle of a circle. Initially, without rotation, the reference line is vertical, connecting the center of the circle to the top of the circumference. Changing the rotation angle of the circle will result in this line being rotated.

```
var Circle = function (center, radius) {
    RigidShape.call(this, center);
    this.mType = "Circle";
    this.mRadius = radius;
    // The start point of line in circle
    this.mStartpoint = new Vec2(center.x, center.y - radius);
};
```

3. Similar to the Rectangle class, you must include the following code to ensure that the Circle class properly inherits from the RigidShape base class.

```
var prototype = Object.create(RigidShape.prototype);
prototype.constructor = Circle;
Circle.prototype = prototype;
```

4. Distinct from that of the rectangle, the arc function of the context is used to draw the circle onto the canvas. In addition, you need to draw the rotation reference line from the center to the mStartpoint, the top of the circle.

```
Circle.prototype.draw = function (context) {
    context.beginPath();
    //draw a circle
    context.arc(this.mCenter.x, this.mCenter.y,
                this.mRadius, 0, Math.PI * 2, true);
    //draw a line from start point toward center
    context.moveTo(this.mStartpoint.x, this.mStartpoint.y);
    context.lineTo(this.mCenter.x, this.mCenter.y);
    context.closePath();
    context.stroke();
};
```

Modify the User Control Script

You will modify the UserControl.js file for testing the new functionality.

1. Edit the UserControl.js file in the SiteRoot (or public_html) folder.

2. Add the gObjectNum variable, an index to the mAllObjects array representing the currently selected object. Notice that this variable is defined before the definition of the userControl function and is a global variable.

    ```
    var gObjectNum = 0;
    ```

3. Within the userControl function, define supports for the creation of random rectangles and circles with the F and G keys.

    ```
    if (keycode === 70) {    // f
        var r1 = new Rectangle(new Vec2(Math.random()*width*0.8,
                                        Math.random()*height*0.8),
                               Math.random() * 30+10,
                               Math.random() * 30+10);
    }
    if (keycode === 71) { //g
        var r1 = new Circle(new Vec2(Math.random()*width*0.8,
                                     Math.random()*height*0.8),
                            Math.random() * 10 + 20);
    }
    ```

4. Within the userControl function, define supports for selecting an object index based on the up/down arrows and the 0 to 9 keys.

    ```
    if (keycode >= 48 && keycode <= 57) {  //number
        if (keycode - 48 < gEngine.Core.mAllObjects.length)
            gObjectNum = keycode - 48;
    }
    if (keycode === 38) {    //up arrow
        if (gObjectNum > 0)
            gObjectNum--;
    }
    if (keycode === 40) {    // down arrow
        if (gObjectNum < gEngine.Core.mAllObjects.length-1)
            gObjectNum++;
    }
    ```

23

Integrate into the Core

You can now modify the Core.js file to integrate and test the newly defined functionality. Your modification will invoke the drawing of all created rigid shapes, and update the User Interface (UI) to properly reflect the state of the application. For now, the drawing will be accomplished through a simple and continuous loop of calling the appropriate drawing functions, or the engine loop. In the next section of this chapter, you will implement a more advanced engine loop to handle the physics engine's calculations.

1. Open Core.js in the Engine Core folder for editing.

2. Create a new runGameLoop function. In runGameLoop, call the windows.requestAnimationFrame to specify the function for the next frame redraw. Additionally, invoke two other functions, the draw and updateUIEcho functions, to draw all the defined rigid shapes and to receive user keyboard entries.

```
var runGameLoop = function () {
    requestAnimationFrame(function () {
        runGameLoop();
    })
    updateUIEcho();
    draw();
};
```

3. Define the updateUIEcho function to update the HTML to display the proper state of the application.

```
var updateUIEcho = function () {
    document.getElementById("uiEchoString").innerHTML =
    "<p><b>Selected Object:</b>:</p>" +
        "<ul style=\"margin:-10px\">" +
        "<li>Id: " + gObjectNum + "</li>" +
        "<li>Center: " + mAllObjects[gObjectNum].mCenter.x.
        toPrecision(3) + "," +
        mAllObjects[gObjectNum].mCenter.y.toPrecision(3) + "</li>" +
        "</ul> <hr>" + "<p><b>Control</b>: of selected object</p>" +
        "<ul style=\"margin:-10px\">" +
        "<li><b>Num</b> or <b>Up/Down Arrow</b>: SelectObject</li>" +
        "</ul> <hr>" +
        "<b>F/G</b>: Spawn [Rectangle/Circle] at random location" + "<hr>";
};
```

4. Add the draw function to iterate through and invoke the corresponding draw functions of the rigid shapes in the mAllObjects list. The strokeStyle property is set such that only the currently selected object is drawn in red while the rest are in blue.

```
var draw = function () {
    mContext.clearRect(0, 0, mWidth, mHeight);
    var i;
    for (i = 0; i < mAllObjects.length; i++) {
        mContext.strokeStyle = 'blue';
        if (i === gObjectNum)
            mContext.strokeStyle = 'red';
        mAllObjects[i].draw(mContext);
    }
};
```

5. Define support to initialize the engine loop when the script runs for the first time.

```
var initializeEngineCore = function () {
    runGameLoop();
};
```

6. Allow public access to the initializeEngineCore function by including it in the mPublic variable.

```
var mPublic = {
    initializeEngineCore: initializeEngineCore,
    mAllObjects: mAllObjects,
    mWidth: mWidth,
    mHeight: mHeight,
    mContext: mContext
};
```

Define the Initial Scene

You can now define a bounded empty environment to test the new functionality.

1. Create a new file under the SiteRoot (or public_html) folder, and name it MyGame.js.

2. Edit this file by creating a new function named MyGame. Inside this function, use the new rigid shape object you just implemented to create the four bounds that define border for future physics simulation.

```
function MyGame() {
    var width = gEngine.Core.mWidth;
    var height = gEngine.Core.mHeight;
    var up = new Rectangle(new Vec2(width / 2, 0), width, 3);
    var down = new Rectangle(new Vec2(width / 2, height), width, 3);
    var left = new Rectangle(new Vec2(0, height / 2), 3, height);
    var right = new Rectangle(new Vec2(width, height / 2), 3, height);
}
```

Note that you can modify the initial scene by editing this function. This can become handy in the following chapters when you want to test the performance of the physics simulation.

Modify the index.html File

To include the new functionality, you need to always remember to include and call them inside the index.html file.

1. Open the index.html file for editing.

2. Modify the body tag to support the handling of keyboard events, define the initial testing environment by instantiating a new MyGame object, and initialize the engine loop by calling the initializeEngineCore.

   ```
   <body onkeydown="return userControl(event);"
       onload="var game = new MyGame();
       gEngine.Core.initializeEngineCore()">
   ```

3. Add a new table row for echoing the application state.

   ```
   <table style="padding: 2px">
       <tr>
           <td>
               <div><canvas id="canvas"></canvas></div>
           </td>
           <td>
               <div id="uiEchoString"> </div>
           </td>
       </tr>
   </table>
   ```

4. Remember to include all the new scripts with the <script> tag.

   ```
   <script type="text/javascript" src="RigidBody/RigidShape.js"></
   script>
   ```

```
<script type="text/javascript" src="RigidBody/Circle.js"></
script>
<script type="text/javascript" src="RigidBody/Rectangle.js">

</script><script type="text/javascript" src="EngineCore/Core.
js"></script>

<script type="text/javascript" src="MyGame.js"></script>
<script type="text/javascript" src="UserControl.js"></script>
```

You can now run the project and test your implementations. It should look like Figure 2-1.

Observation

You can now run the project to test your implementation. Notice the four bounding borders and the text output to the right that prints instructions for the user and echoes the application state, which includes the index of the selected object. Pressing the F or G key generates a rectangle or circle at a random position with a random size. This drawing simulation seems rather similar to the previous project. The main differences are in the object abstraction and drawing mechanism—RigidShape class definition and engine loop monitoring user input and drawing of all defined objects. In the next project you will evolve the engine loop to support the changing of rigid shape states, including allowing the user to change the attributes of each of the rigid shapes in the scene and simple simulation of falling objects.

The Core Engine Loop

One of the most important characteristics of any physics engine is the support of seemingly intuitive and continuous interactions between the objects and the graphical simulation elements. In reality, these interactions are implemented as a continuous running loop that receives and processes the calculations, updates the object states, and renders the objects. This constantly running loop is referred to as the *engine loop*.

To convey the proper sense of intuitiveness, each cycle of the engine loop must be completed within a normal human's reaction time. This is often referred to as *real time*, which is the amount of time that is too short for humans to detect visually. Typically, real-time can be achieved when the engine loop is running at a rate of higher than 40 to 60 cycles in a second. Since there is often one drawing operation in each loop cycle, the loop cycle's rate can also be expressed as frames per second (FPS), or the *frame rate*. An FPS of 60 is a good target for performance. This is to say, your engine must process calculations, update the object states, and then draw the canvas all within 1/60th of a second!

The loop itself, including the implementation details, is the most fundamental control structure for an engine. With the main goal of maintaining real-time performance, the details of an engine loop's operation are of no concern to the rest of the physics engine. For this reason, the implementation of an engine loop should be tightly encapsulated in the core of the engine, with its detailed operations hidden from other elements.

Engine Loop Implementations

An engine loop is the mechanism through which logic and drawing are continuously executed. A simple engine loop consists of processing the input, updating the state of objects, and drawing those objects, as illustrated in the following pseudocode:

```
initialize();
while(game running) {
    input();
    update();
    draw();
}
```

As discussed, an FPS of 60 or higher is ideal to maintain the sense of real-time interactivity. When the game complexity increases, one problem that may arise is when sometimes a single loop can take longer than 1/60th of a second to complete, causing the game to run at a reduced frame rate. When this happens, the entire game will appear to slow down. A common solution is to prioritize which operations to emphasis and which to skip. Since correct input and updates are required for an engine to function as designed, it is often the draw operation that is skipped when necessary. This is referred to as *frame skipping*, and the following pseudocode illustrates one such implementation:

```
elapsedTime = now;
previousLoop = now;
while(game running) {
    elapsedTime += now - previousLoop;
    previousLoop = now;

    input();
    while( elapsedTime >= UPDATE_TIME_RATE ) {
        update();
        elapsedTime -= UPDATE_TIME_RATE;
    }
    draw();
}
```

In the previous pseudocode listing, UPDATE_TIME_RATE is the required real-time update rate. When the elapsed time between the engine loop cycle is greater than the UPDATE_TIME_RATE, the update function will be called until it is caught up. This means that the draw operation is essentially skipped when the engine loop is running too slowly. When this happens, the entire game will appear to run slowly, with lagging play input response and frames skipped. However, the game logic will continue to be correct.

Notice that the while loop that encompasses the update function call simulates a fixed update time step of UPDATE_TIME_RATE. This fixed time step update allows for a straightforward implementation in maintaining a deterministic game state.

The Core Engine Loop Project

This project demonstrates how to incorporate a loop into your engine and to support real-time simulation by updating and drawing the objects accordingly. You can see an example of this project running in Figure 2-3. The source code to this project is defined in

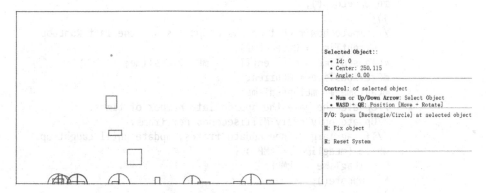

Figure 2-3. *Running the Core Engine Loop Project*

the Core Engine Loop Project folder.

The goals of the project are as follows:

- To understand the internal operations of an engine loop.

- To implement and encapsulate the operations of an engine loop.

- To gain experience with continuous update and draw to simulate animation.

Implement the Engine Loop Component

The engine loop component is a core engine functionality and thus should be implemented as a property of the gEngine.Core. The actual implementation is similar to the pseudocode listing discussed.

1. Edit the Core.js file.

2. Add the necessary variables to determine the loop frequency.

```
var mCurrentTime, mElapsedTime, mPreviousTime = Date.now(),
mLagTime = 0;
var kFPS = 60;            // Frames per second
var kFrameTime = 1 / kFPS;
var mUpdateIntervalInSeconds = kFrameTime;
var kMPF = 1000 * kFrameTime; // Milliseconds per frame.
```

3. Update the runGameLoop function to keep track of the elapsed time between frames and to ensure that the update function is called at the frame rate frequency.

```
var runGameLoop = function () {
    requestAnimationFrame(function () {
    runGameLoop();
    });
    //compute how much time has elapsed since the last RunLoop
    mCurrentTime = Date.now();
    mElapsedTime = mCurrentTime - mPreviousTime;
    mPreviousTime = mCurrentTime;
    mLagTime += mElapsedTime;
    //Update the game the appropriate number of times.
    //Update only every Milliseconds per frame.
    //If lag larger then update frames, update until caught up.
    while (mLagTime >= kMPF) {
        mLagTime -= kMPF;
        update();
    }
    updateUIEcho();
    draw();
};
```

4. Modify the updateUIEcho function to print out additional relevant application state information, like how to rotate and move the selected rigid shape. The code in bold is the only addition to the function.

```
var updateUIEcho = function () {
    document.getElementById("uiEchoString").innerHTML =
    // ... identical to previous project
    mAllObjects[gObjectNum].mCenter.y.toPrecision(3) + "</li>" +
        "<li>Angle: " + mAllObjects[gObjectNum].mAngle.
        toPrecision(3) + "</li>" +
    "</ul> <hr>" +
    "<p><b>Control</b>: of selected object</p>" +
    "<ul style=\"margin:-10px\">" +
        "<li><b>Num</b> or <b>Up/Down Arrow</b>: SelectObject</
        li>" +
        "<li><b>WASD</b> + <b>QE</b>: Position [Move + Rotate]</
        li>" +
    "</ul> <hr>" +
    "<b>F/G</b>: Spawn [Rectangle/Circle] at selected object" +
    "<p><b>H</b>: Fix object</p>" +
    "<p><b>R</b>: Reset System</p>" +
    "<hr>";
};
```

5. Create a new function named update, which will call the update function of every rigid shape defined.

```
var update = function () {
    var i;
    for (i = 0; i < mAllObjects.length; i++) {
        mAllObjects[i].update(mContext);
    }
};
```

Extend the Rigid Shape Classes

You are going to modify the rigid shape base class, and both of the Rectangle and Circle classes to support the implementation of simple behavior. While the update function is defined in the rigid shape base class to be invoked by the game engine loop, the detailed implementation of update must necessarily be subclass-specific. For instance, a circle object implements moving behavior by changing the values in its center while a rectangle object must change all of the values in the vertex and face normal arrays to simulate the same movement behavior.

Rigid Shape Base Class

1. Edit the RigidShape.js file.

2. Define the update function to be called by the engine loop and implement the simple falling behavior by changing the center position with a constant y-direction vector. Notice that the free fall behavior is only applied when the shape is within the vertical bounds of the canvas.

```
RigidShape.prototype.update = function () {
    if (this.mCenter.y < gEngine.Core.mHeight && this.mFix !== 0)
        this.move(new Vec2(0, 1));
};
```

Subclasses are responsible for defining the mFix variable and the move function to control if the shape is fixed where it should not follow the falling behavior and to implement the moving of the shape. It should be emphasized that this rigid shape movement behavior is included here for testing purposes only and will be removed in the next project. Actual physics-based movement of rigid shape objects and the associated physical quantities (including velocity and acceleration) will be introduced and discussed in Chapter 4.

Note that by default the canvas coordinate defines the origin, (0, 0), to be located at the top left corner, and positive y direction to be downwards. For this reason, to simulate gravity, you will move all objects in the positive y direction.

The Circle Class

The Circle class is modified to implement movements.

1. Edit the Circle.js file.

2. Define the mFix instance variable to enable or disable the falling behavior.

```
var Circle = function (center, radius, fix) {
    // ... code similar to previous project
    this.mFix = fix;
    // ... code similar to previous project
```

3. Add a move function to define how a circle is moved by a vector—adding the movement vector to the center and the mStartpoint.

```
Circle.prototype.move = function (s) {
    this.mStartpoint = this.mStartpoint.add(s);
    this.mCenter = this.mCenter.add(s);
        return this;
};
```

4. Add rotate function to implement the rotation of a circle. Note that since a circle is infinitely symmetrical, a rotated circle would appear identical to the original shape. The mStartpoint position allows a rotated reference line to be drawn to indicate angle of rotation of a circle.

```
// rotate angle in counterclockwise
Circle.prototype.rotate = function (angle) {
    this.mAngle += angle;
    this.mStartpoint = this.mStartpoint.rotate(this.mCenter, angle);
    return this;
};
```

The Rectangle Class

Similar to the circle class, the Rectangle class must be modified to support the new functionality.

1. Edit the Rectangle.js file.

2. Define the mFix instance variable to enable or disable the falling behavior.

```
var Rectangle = function (center, width, height, fix) {
    // ... code similar to previous project
    this.mFix = fix;
    // ... code similar to previous project
```

3. Define the move function by changing the values of all vertices and the center.

```
Rectangle.prototype.move = function (v) {
    var i;
    for (i = 0; i < this.mVertex.length; i++) {
        this.mVertex[i] = this.mVertex[i].add(v);
    }
    this.mCenter = this.mCenter.add(v);
    return this;
};
```

4. Define the rotate function by rotating all over the vertices and recomputing the face normals.

```
Rectangle.prototype.rotate = function (angle) {
    this.mAngle += angle;
    var i;
    for (i = 0; i < this.mVertex.length; i++) {
        this.mVertex[i] = this.mVertex[i].rotate(this.mCenter,
        angle);
    }
    this.mFaceNormal[0] = this.mVertex[1].subtract(this.
    mVertex[2]);
    this.mFaceNormal[0] = this.mFaceNormal[0].normalize();
    this.mFaceNormal[1] = this.mVertex[2].subtract(this.
    mVertex[3]);
    this.mFaceNormal[1] = this.mFaceNormal[1].normalize();
    this.mFaceNormal[2] = this.mVertex[3].subtract(this.
    mVertex[0]);
    this.mFaceNormal[2] = this.mFaceNormal[2].normalize();
    this.mFaceNormal[3] = this.mVertex[0].subtract(this.
    mVertex[1]);
    this.mFaceNormal[3] = this.mFaceNormal[3].normalize();
    return this;
};
```

Modify User Control Script

You will need to extend the userControl function defined in the UserControl.js file to support movements, rotation, disable/enable gravity, and reset the entire scene.

1. Edit the UserControl.js file.

2. Add statements to support moving, rotating, and toggling of gravity on the selected object.

```
// move with WASD keys
if (keycode === 87) { //W
    gEngine.Core.mAllObjects[gObjectNum].move(new Vec2(0, -10));
}
if (keycode === 83) { // S
    gEngine.Core.mAllObjects[gObjectNum].move(new Vec2(0, +10));
}
if (keycode === 65) { //A
    gEngine.Core.mAllObject[gObjectNum].move(new Vec2(-10, 0));
}
if (keycode === 68) { //D
    gEngine.Core.mAllObjects[gObjectNum].move(new Vec2(10, 0));
}

// Rotate with QE keys
if (keycode === 81) { //Q
    gEngine.Core.mAllObjects[gObjectNum].rotate(-0.1);
}
if (keycode === 69) { //E
    gEngine.Core.mAllObjects[gObjectNum].rotate(0.1);
}

// Toggle gravity with the H key
if (keycode === 72) { //H
    if(gEngine.Core.mAllObjects[gObjectNum].mFix === 0)
        gEngine.Core.mAllObjects[gObjectNum].mFix = 1;
    else gEngine.Core.mAllObjects[gObjectNum].mFix = 0;
}
```

3. Add a statement to reset the scene.

```
if (keycode === 82) { //R
    gEngine.Core.mAllObjects.splice(5, gEngine.Core.mAllObjects.
    length);
    gObjectNum = 0;
}
```

4. Modify object creation statements of the G and F keys such
    that the new object is created at the location of the currently
    selected object, rather than a random position.

```
if (keycode === 70) { //f
    var r1 = new Rectangle(new Vec2(gEngine.Core.
    mAllObjects[gObjectNum].mCenter.x,
    gEngine.Core.mAllObjects[gObjectNum].mCenter.y),
    Math.random() * 30 + 10, Math.random() * 30 + 10);
}
if (keycode === 71) { //g
    var r1 = new Circle(new Vec2(gEngine.Core.
    mAllObjects[gObjectNum].mCenter.x,
    gEngine.Core.mAllObjects[gObjectNum].mCenter.y),
    Math.random() * 10 + 20);
}
```

Update the Scene

To test the implemented engine loop and object movements, you will create an initial
selected object to the scene. This initial object will serve as the cursor position for
spawning created rigid shapes. This can be accomplished by editing the MyGame.js file
and creating an initial object

```
function MyGame() {
    var width = gEngine.Core.mWidth;
    var height = gEngine.Core.mHeight;
    var r1 = new Rectangle(new Vec2(width / 2, height / 2), 3, 3, 0);

    var up = new Rectangle(new Vec2(width / 2, 0), width, 3, 0);
    var down = new Rectangle(new Vec2(width / 2, height), width, 3, 0);
    var left = new Rectangle(new Vec2(0, height / 2), 3, height, 0);
    var right = new Rectangle(new Vec2(width, height / 2), 3, height, 0);
}
```

Observation

Run the project to test your implementation. You will see that the scene is almost the same
as that of the previous project except for the small initial cursor object. See that you can
change the selected object, and thereby the cursor object, with the 0 to 9, or the up and
down arrow keys. Type F and G keys to see that new objects are created at the cursor object
location and they always follow the falling behavior. This real-time smooth falling behavior
indicates that the engine loop has been successfully implemented. You can play around
with the selected shape position using the WASD, QE, and H keys; and move, rotate, and
toggle gravity on the selected object. You may also notice that without movement of the
cursor object, the newly created objects are clustered together, which can be confusing.

That is because the physics simulation has yet to be defined. In the next chapter you will learn about and implement collision detection as a first step to remedy the clustered object problem.

Summary

In this chapter, you have implemented basic rigid shape classes. Although only simple position, orientation, and drawing are supported, these classes represent a well-defined abstraction, hide implementation details, and thus support future integration of complexity. In the following chapters, you will learn about other physical quantities including mass, inertia, friction, and restitution. The engine loop project introduced you to the basics of a continuous update loop that supports real time per-shape computation and enables visually appealing physics simulations. In the next chapter, you will begin learning about physics simulation by first examining the collision between rigid shapes in detail.

CHAPTER 3

■ ■ ■

Incorporating Collision Detection

In the context of 2D video games, the fundamentals of a physical simulation involves movements of rigid shapes, collisions of the moving shapes, and responses after the collisions. In the previous chapter, you defined the rigid shape classes and a core engine loop to support basic drawing, update operations, and simple movements of rigid shapes. In this chapter, you will learn about and implement the detection of rigid shape collisions and compute the necessary information, such that in the next chapter you can begin resolving and implementing the responses to the collisions. The proper implementation based on these concepts enables believable scenarios when objects physically interact with each other in the simulated world.

This chapter focuses on the foundations of detecting collisions, including how to approximate the detection, a theory for exact detection of colliding rectangles and circles in any orientations, and essential information to capture after detecting a collision to support resolution of interpenetration and proper responses to collisions. You will implement this system in a step-by-step manner, from a simple broad phase collision detection method, to the more accurate and computationally more costly Separating Axis Theorem (SAT). In this way, at each step the collision detection will become more accurate and be applicable to more general cases until your solution is ready to be used in the next chapter for resolving and responding to collisions. The final result of this chapter will be a collision detection system that can detect collisions between rigid rectangles and circles of any size and in orientations where the information required for resolving and responding to the collisions are computed and available.

After completing this chapter, you will be able to:

- Appreciate the significant computational cost of detecting object collisions.

- Optimize object collision detection with broad phase collisions to avoid unnecessary computations.

- Understand that, in a computer simulation, rigid bodies can interpenetrate during a collision and that this interpenetration must be resolved.

© Michael Tanaya, Huaming Chen, Jebediah Pavleas and Kelvin Sung 2017
M. Tanaya et al., *Building a 2D Game Physics Engine*, DOI 10.1007/978-1-4842-2583-7_3

- Learn and use the Separating Axis Theorem (SAT) to detect rigid body collisions.

- Compute the necessary information to support efficient positional correction. In the next chapter, you will learn about effective resolution of rigid body interpenetration using this computed information.

- Implement an efficient collision detection algorithm that is based on SAT.

- Detect collisions between rigid rectangles and circles accurately.

Interpenetration of Colliding Objects

As illustrated in Figure 3-1, the fixed update time step introduced in the previous chapter means object positions in continuous motion are approximated by a discrete set of positions. The most notable ramifications of these approximations are in detecting collisions.

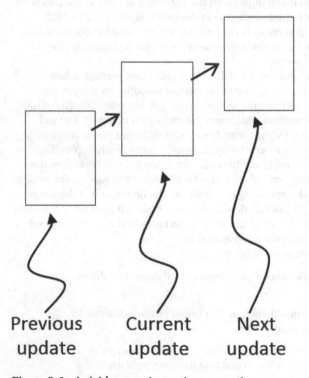

Previous update   Current update   Next update

Figure 3-1. A rigid square in continuous motion

You can see one such problem in Figure 3-1; imagine a thin wall existed in the space between the current and the next update. You would expect the object to collide and stop by the wall in the next update. However, if the wall were thin enough, the object would essentially pass right through it as it jumped from one position to the next. This is a common problem faced in many game engines. A general solution for these types of problems can be algorithmically complex and computationally intensive. It is typically the job of the game designer to mitigate and avoid this problem with well-designed (for example, appropriate size) and well-behaved (for example, appropriate traveling speed) game objects.

Figure 3-2 shows two objects colliding after a time step. Before the time step, the objects are not touching. However, after the time step, the results of the movement simulation place the two objects over each other.

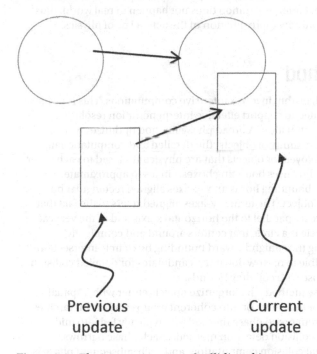

Previous
update

Current
update

Figure 3-2. *The interpenetration of colliding objects*

This is another example ramification of fixed update time step with discrete intervals. In the real world, given that the objects were solid, the two would never interpenetrate. This is where details of a collision must be computed such that the interpenetrating situation can be properly resolved.

Collision Detection

Collision detection is a vital and potentially a costly piece of physics simulations that can impact performance significantly. For example, if you want to detect the collisions between five objects, in the worst case you must perform four detection computations for the first objects, followed by three computations for the second, two for the third, and one for the fourth. In general, without dedicated optimizations, in the worst case you must perform $O(N^2)$ operations to detect the collisions between N objects.

In addition to reporting if a collision has occurred, a collision detection algorithm should also support the computation of information that can be used to resolve and respond to the collision. This information can include penetration depth, and the normal vector of penetration. It is important to compute this information accurately such that the collision can be effectively resolved and the response properly computed to simulate the real world. Remember that object interpenetration does not happen in real world, thus the computed information are only an approximation of the actual law of physics.

Broad Phase Method

A detailed collision detection algorithm involves intensive computations. This is because accurate results must be computed to support effective interpenetration resolution and realistic collision response simulation. A broad phase method optimizes this computation by exploiting the proximity of objects: the detailed and computationally intensive algorithm are only deployed for objects that are physically closed to each other.

A popular broad phase method uses bounding boxes/circles to approximate collisions between all objects. A bounding box is an x/y-axes aligned rectangular box that completely bounds a given object. The term x/y-axes aligned refers to the fact that the four sides of a bounding box are parallel to the horizontal x-axis and to the vertical y-axis. Similarly, a bounding circle is a circle that centers around and completely bounds an object. By performing the straightforward bounding box/circle intersection computations, it becomes possible to narrow down the candidates for detailed collision detection operations to only those with colliding bounds.

There are other broad phase methods that organize objects either with a spatial structure such as uniform grid or quad-tree or into coherent groups such as hierarchies of bounding colliders. Results from broad phase methods are typically fed into mid phase and finally narrow phase collision detection methods. Each phase narrows down candidates for the eventual collision computation, and each subsequent phase is incrementally more accurate and more expensive.

This chapter only introduces you to the bounding circle broad phase collision method followed by a narrow phase algorithm that is based on the Separation Axis Theorem (SAT).

The Broad Phase Method Project

This project demonstrates how to implement a broad phase collision detection method using bounding circles. You can see an example of this project running in Figure 3-3. The source code to this project is defined in the Broad Phase Method Project folder.

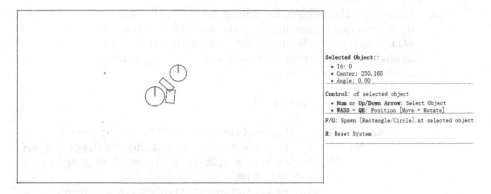

Figure 3-3. *Running the Broad Phase Method Project*

Project goals:

- To understand the implementation of bounding circle collision detection.

- To understand the strengths and weaknesses of broad phase collision detection.

- To lay the foundation for building a narrow phase collision detection algorithm.

Define the Physics Engine Component

A physics engine component can now be defined to support the collision detection computations. To begin, follow the steps of defining an engine component.

1. In the SiteRoot/EngineCore (or public_html/EngineCore) folder, create a new file and name it Physics.js. This file will implement the physics engine component. Remember to load this new source file in index.html.

2. Define the physics component in a similar fashion as you defined gEngine.Core:

```
var gEngine = gEngine || { };
gEngine.Physics = (function () {
    var mPublic = {
    };
    return mPublic;
}());
```

3. Create a collision function within gEngine.Physics to test
    the intersection of bounding circles between all objects in the
    mAllObjects list. Notice the nested loops that test every object
    against each other for collision and that the colliding objects
    are drawn with green color.

```
var collision = function () {
    var i, j;
    for (i = 5; i < gEngine.Core.mAllObjects.length; i++) {
        for (j = i + 1; j < gEngine.Core.mAllObjects.length; j++){
            If (gEngine.Core.mAllObjects[i].boundTest(gEngine.
                Core.mAllObjects[j])) {
                gEngine.Core.mContext.strokeStyle = 'green';
                gEngine.Core.mAllObjects[i].draw(gEngine.Core.
                mContext);
                gEngine.Core.mAllObjects[j].draw(gEngine.Core.
                mContext);
            }
        }
    }
};
```

4. Add public variable within mPublic to allow access to the
    collision function.

```
var mPublic = {
    collision: collision
};
```

Invoke the Physics Collision and Update the UI

Edit the Core.js file in the SiteRoot/EngineCore (or public_html/EngineCore) folder.

1. Invoke the collision computation from the runGameLoop
    function within the core engine loop.

```
//....identical to previous project
while (mLagTime >= kMPF) {
    mLagTime -= kMPF;
    gEngine.Physics.collision();
    update();
}
//....identical to previous project
```

2. Modify the updateUIEcho function to remove support for the H button. The gravity on/off functionality is no longer required.

```
//...identical to previous project
"<b>F/G</b>: Spawn [Rectangle/Circle] at selected object" +
"<p><b>H</b>: Fix object</p>" + // remove this line
"<p><b>R</b>: Reset System</p>" +
```

Modify Rigid Shape Classes

Now you can modify all the files inside the rigid shape folder to support a bounding circle test for the broad phase collision detection method.

1. You need to modify rigid shape base class. Open RigidShape.js under the folder SiteRoot/RigidBody (or public_html/RigidBody).

2. Add the mBoundRadius variable to the RigidShape constructor. This is the radius of the bounding circle for the rigid shape.

```
this.mBoundRadius = 0;
```

3. Define a new prototype function, and name it boundTest, a function that will test if two bounding circles have collided. The most straightforward way to detect the collision between two circles is to determine if the distance between the two centers is less than the sum of the radii. The scenario is depicted in Figure 3-4.

```
RigidShape.prototype.boundTest = function (otherShape) {
    var vFrom1to2 = otherShape.mCenter.subtract(this.mCenter);
    var rSum = this.mBoundRadius + otherShape.mBoundRadius;
    var dist = vFrom1to2.length();
    if (dist > rSum) {
        return false;  //not overlapping
    }
    return true;
};
```

43

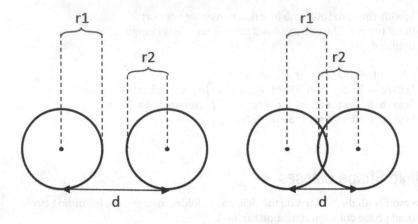

(a) No collision (d>r1+r2)   **(b) Collision (d<r1+r2)**

Figure 3-4. *Circle collision detection: (a) no collision (b) collision detected*

4. You also need to remove the movement testing code that was defined as the update function of the RigidShape base class.

```
RigidShape.prototype.update = function () { };
```

5. Next, modify the Circle.js file in the same folder to initialize the value for the mBoundRadius variable in the constructor. The bounding circle of a rigid circle shape has the same radius as the rigid shape. Remember to remove the mFix variable.

```
this.mBoundRadius = radius;
this.mFix = fix; //remove this line
```

6. Modify the Rectangle.js file for a similar purpose, to initialize the mBoundRadius variable in the constructor. In this case, the bounding circle for a rectangle rigid shape is defined as half of the diagonal distance of the rectangle. Once again, remember to remove the unused mFix variable.

```
this.mBoundRadius = Math.sqrt(width*width + height*height)/2;
```

Observation

Run the project to test your implementation. Notice that by default, objects are created in the same location, have bounding circles that overlap, and thus are drawn in a green color. You can select an object and move/rotate it to observe the green color changing back to black when there are no overlaps of their corresponding bounding circles. Now, create a rectangle and a circle, and move them apart. Rotate the rectangle and move it close to, but without actually touching, the circle. You may notice that the two shapes are not touching and yet both are drawn in green. That is because the collision bound for the rectangle is a circle, which overestimates the bounds of the object as shown in Figure 3-5. This is the most important drawback with this broad phase method: though efficient, it is inaccurate. This issue will be remedied by the SAT algorithm to be introduced in a later section.

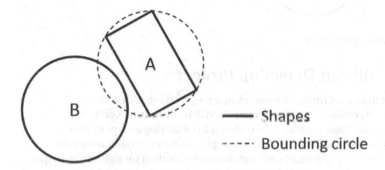

Figure 3-5. False positive collision between Rectangle-A and Circle-B

Collision Information

With the broad phase collision method implemented, you can now begin the process of defining narrow phase methods for detecting the collision between different rigid shapes. As discussed earlier, information regarding the specifics of a collision must be computed to support proper resolution of interpenetration and response. As illustrated in Figure 3-6, the essential information of a collision includes: collision depth, normal, start, and end. The collision depth is the smallest amount that the objects interpenetrated where the collision normal is the direction along which the collision depth is measured. The start and end are beginning and end positions of the interpenetration defined for the convenience of drawing the interpenetration as a line segment. It is always true that any interpenetration can be resolved by moving the colliding objects along the collision normal by the collision depth distance from the start to the end position.

This section leads you to develop the infrastructure for computing and working with collision information based on collisions between rigid circle shapes—a straightforward extension to the previous project. After this section, with the proper support for storing and accessing collision information, the Separating Axis Theorem (SAT) will be introduced and implemented.

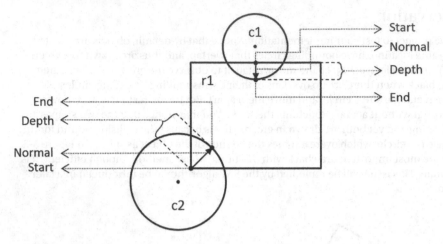

Figure 3-6. *Collision information*

The Circle Collision Detection Project

This project builds the infrastructure for computing and working with collision information based on collisions between circles. As will be discussed, collision information records the specific details of a collision for resolving interpenetration and generating responses. Notice that the bounding circle-based broad phase collision detection method computes the exact collision detection solution for rigid circle shapes. For this reason, this project can take advantage of the previous project and focus on computing and working with collision information. You can see an example of this project running in Figure 3-7. The source code to this project is defined in the Circle Collision Detection Project folder.

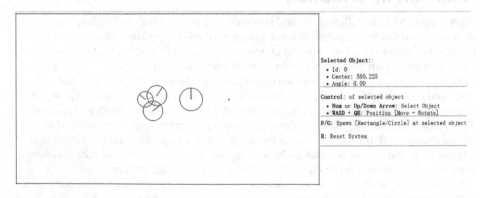

Figure 3-7. *Running the Circle Collision Detection Project*

Project goals:

- To define collision information.

- To build the infrastructure for computing and working with collision information.

- To compute and display collision information for circles.

Define Collision Information Object

A new class must be defined to support the storage of collision information.

1. Under the SiteRoot/Lib (or public_html/Lib) folder, create a new file and name it CollisionInfo.js. Remember to load this new source file in index.html.

2. Define the constructor of the object to contain collision depth, collision normal, and a start and end positions. These are the beginning and ending positions of a collision interpenetration.

```
function CollisionInfo() {
    this.mDepth = 0;
    this.mNormal = new Vec2(0, 0);
    this.mStart = new Vec2(0, 0);
    this.mEnd = new Vec2(0, 0);
}
```

3. Define the getter and setter for the object.

```
CollisionInfo.prototype.setNormal = function (s) {
    this.mNormal = s;
};

CollisionInfo.prototype.getDepth = function () {
    return this.mDepth;
};

CollisionInfo.prototype.getNormal = function () {
    return this.mNormal;
};

CollisionInfo.prototype.setInfo = function (d, n, s) {
    this.mDepth = d;
    this.mNormal = n;
    this.mStart = s;
    this.mEnd = s.add(n.scale(d));
};
```

4. Create a function to change the direction of the normal. This function will be used to ensure that the normal is always pointing from the primary to the object that is being tested for collision.

```
CollisionInfo.prototype.changeDir = function () {
    this.mNormal = this.mNormal.scale(-1);
    var n = this.mStart;
    this.mStart = this.mEnd;
    this.mEnd = n;
};
```

Compute Collision Information Between Two Circles

In the previous project you implemented the functionality for detecting collisions between two circles. In the following, you will amend the computation of collision information to include the information gained from circle collisions.

1. Create a new file under the SiteRoot/RigidBody (or public_html/RigidBody) folder, and name it Circle_collision.js. This file will contain the implementation of colliding a rigid circle shape with other rigid shapes.

2. Define the collisionTest function to collide a rigid circle shape with another RigidShape object. Notice that the actual collision testing function is shape-specific. For now, a circle only knows how to collide with a circle and will always return false for any other shapes.

```
Circle.prototype.collisionTest = function (otherShape,
collisionInfo) {
    var status = false;
    if (otherShape.mType === "Circle")
        status = this.collidedCircCirc(this, otherShape,
        collisionInfo);
    else
        status = false;
    return status;
};
```

3. Define the collideCircCirc function to detect the collision between two circles and to compute the corresponding collision information when a collision is detected. There are three cases to the collision detection: no collision, collision with centers of the two circles located at different, and at exactly the same positions. The following code shows the detection of no collision. The details are depicted in Figure 3-8; vFrom1to2 is the vector pointing from center of c1 to center of c2, rSum is the sum of the radii, and dist is the distance between the centers of two circles.

```
Circle.prototype.collidedCircCirc = function (c1, c2,
collisionInfo) {
    var vFrom1to2 = c2.mCenter.subtract(c1.mCenter);
    var rSum = c1.mRadius + c2.mRadius;
    var dist = vFrom1to2.length();
    if (dist > Math.sqrt(rSum * rSum)) {
        return false; //not overlapping
    }
    // ... details in the following steps
};
```

4. A collision is detected when dist, the distance between the centers of the two circles, is less than the sum of the radii. In this case, if the two circles do not have centers located at the exact same position, the collision depth and normal can be computed. As illustrated in Figure 3-8, since c2 is the reference to the other RigidShape, the collision normal is a vector pointing from c1 towards c2, or in the same direction as vFrom1to2. The collision depth is the difference between rSum and dist, and the start position for c1 is simple c2's radius distance away from the center of c2 along the normalFrom2to1 direction.

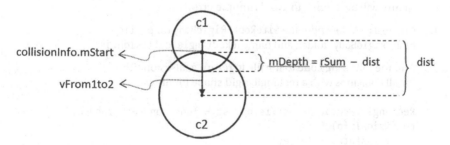

Figure 3-8. Details of a circle-circle collision

```
//... continue from the previous step
if (dist !== 0) {
    // overlapping but not same position
    var normalFrom2to1 = vFrom1to2.scale(-1).normalize();
    var radiusC2 = normalFrom2to1.scale(c2.mRadius);
    collisionInfo.setInfo(rSum - dist, vFrom1to2.normalize(),
        c2.mCenter.add(radiusC2));
}
//... details in the next step
```

5. The last case for two colliding circles is when both circles'
    centers are located at exactly the same position. In this case,
    as shown in the following code, the collision normal is defined
    to be the negative y-direction, and the collision depth is
    simply the larger of the two radii.

```
//...continue from the previous step
if (dist !== 0) {
    //...identical to previous step
} else {
    //same position
    if (c1.mRadius > c2.mRadius)
        collisionInfo.setInfo(rSum, new Vec2(0, -1),
                    c1.mCenter.add(new Vec2(0, c1.mRadius)));
    else
        collisionInfo.setInfo(rSum, new Vec2(0, -1),
                    c2.mCenter.add(new Vec2(0, c2.mRadius)));
}
```

Case for Collision with a Rectangle

The collision computations for a rectangle will be covered later in this chapter. For now,
an empty structure will be defined to avoid runtime errors.

1. Create a new file under the SiteRoot/RigidBody (or public_
    html/RigidBody) folder, and name it Rectangle_collision.js.

2. Add the following code to the file to return a false condition
    for all collisions with a rectangle rigid shape for now.

```
Rectangle.prototype.collisionTest = function (otherShape,
collisionInfo) {
    var status = false;
    if (otherShape.mType === "Circle")
        status = false;
```

```
    else
        status = false;
    return status;
};
```

Modify Physics Engine Component

You can now modify the physics component to support the computation of collision information when computing circle-to-circle collisions.

1. Edit EngineCore/Physics.js to support the drawing of collision information and to call the newly defined rigid shape collisionTest function.

2. For debugging and testing purposes, define the drawCollisionInfo function to draw the collision depth and normal as an orange colored line over the rigid shape.

```
var drawCollisionInfo = function (collisionInfo, context) {
    context.beginPath();
    context.moveTo(collisionInfo.mStart.x, collisionInfo.
    mStart.y);
    context.lineTo(collisionInfo.mEnd.x, collisionInfo.mEnd.y);
    context.closePath();
    context.strokeStyle = "orange";
    context.stroke();
};
```

3. In the collision function, first create a collisionInfo object to record the details of collisions. After the broad phase boundTest returns true, the details for the collision must be determined by calling the rigid shape collisionTest function you just defined.

```
//....identical to previous project
var collisionInfo = new CollisionInfo();
for (i = 0; i < gEngine.Core.mAllObjects.length; i++) {
    for (j = i + 1; j < gEngine.Core.mAllObjects.length; j++) {
        if (gEngine.Core.mAllObjects[i].boundTest(gEngine.Core.
        mAllObjects[j])) {
            if (gEngine.Core.mAllObjects[i].collisionTest(gEngine.
            Core.mAllObjects[j], collisionInfo)) {
                // ... details in the next step
            }
        }
    }
//....identical to previous project
```

4. When a collision is deemed valid, it is important to ensure that the collision normal is always in the direction towards the object being tested. As illustrated in the following code, this can be determined by the sign of the dot product between the collision normal and the vector defined by the centers of the colliding objects. drawCollisionInfo function is called to draw the corresponding collision information.

```
//... continue from the previous step
if (gEngine.Core.mAllObjects[i].collisionTest(gEngine.Core.
mAllObjects[j], collisionInfo)) {
    //make sure the normal is always from object[i] to object[j]
    if (collisionInfo.getNormal().dot(
        gEngine.Core.mAllObjects[j].mCenter.subtract({
        gEngine.Core.mAllObject[i].mCenter)) < 0) {
            collisionInfo.changeDir();
            }
    //draw collision info (a black line that shows normal)
    drawCollisionInfo(collisionInfo, gEngine.Core.mContext);
}
//... identical to previous project
```

Observation

Run the project to test your implementation. Notice that when you create two circles, their collision is no longer indicated by a change of color. Instead, orange lines are drawn inside the colliding circles to indicate the corresponding collision depth and normal. You can create and observe the collision information drawn on all colliding circles. The collision information will be used to resolve collision interpenetrations. Lastly, observe that collision information is absent from rigid rectangle shapes. This is because you have not implemented the functionality and the corresponding collisionTest function always returns false. The next two projects will guide you through the implementation of collision computation between rigid rectangle shape.

Separating Axis Theorem

The Separating Axis Theorem (SAT) is the foundation for one of the most popular algorithms used for detecting collision between general convex shapes in 2D. Since the derived algorithm can be overly computationally intensive for real-time systems, it is typically preceded with an initial pass of broad phase method, as introduced in the previous section. The SAT states that:

Two convex polygons are not colliding if there exists a line (or axis) that is perpendicular to one of the given edges of the two polygons and when projecting all edges of the two polygons onto this axis results in no overlaps of the projected edges.

In other words, given two convex shapes in 2D space, you can iterate through all of the edges of the convex shapes, one at a time. For each of the edges, compute a line (or axis) that is perpendicular to the edge, project all edges of the two convex shapes onto this line, and compute for overlaps of the projected edges. If you can find one of the perpendicular lines where none of the projected edges overlaps, then the two convex shapes do not collide.

Figure 3-9 illustrates this description using two axes-aligned rectangles. In this case, there are two lines that are perpendicular to the two given shapes, the X and Y axes.

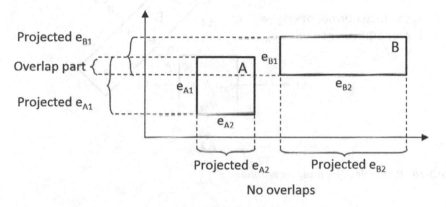

Figure 3-9. There exists a projection that does not overlap

When projecting all of the shape edges onto these two lines, note that the projection results on the Y-axis overlaps, while there is no overlap on the X-axis. Since there exists one line that is perpendicular to one of the rectangle edges where the projected edges do not overlap, the SAT concludes that the two given rectangles do not collide.

The main strength of algorithms derived from the SAT is that for non-colliding shapes, it has an early exit capability. As soon as an axis with no overlapping projected edges is detected, an algorithm can report no collision and does not need to continue with the testing for other axes. In the case of Figure 3-9, if the algorithm began with processing the X-axis, there would be no need to perform the computation for the Y-axis.

A Simple SAT-based Algorithm

Algorithms derived based on the SAT typically consist of four steps:

- **Step 1 Compute Face Normals**: Compute the perpendicular axes, or face normals for projecting the edges. As illustrated in Figure 3-10, a rectangle has four edges and each edge has a corresponding perpendicular axis. For example, A1 is the corresponding axis for and thus is perpendicular to the edge e_{A1}. Note that in your rigid rectangle implementation, mFaceNormal, or face normals, are the perpendicular axes A1, A2, A3, and A4.

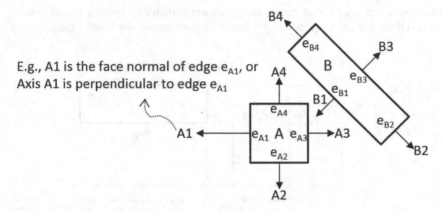

Figure 3-10. Rectangle edges and face normals

- **Step 2 Project Vertices**: Project each of the vertices of the two convex shapes onto the face normals. Figure 3-11 illustrates this projection of all vertices onto the A1 axis from Figure 3-10.

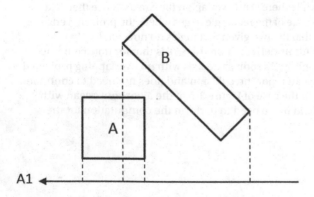

Figure 3-11. Project each vertex onto face normals (example shows A1)

- **Step 3 Identify Bounds:** Identify the min and max bounds for the projected vertices of each convex shape. Continue with the previous rectangle example. Figure 3-12 shows identifying the min and max positions for each of the two rectangles. Notice that the min/max positions are defined with respect to the direction of the given axis.

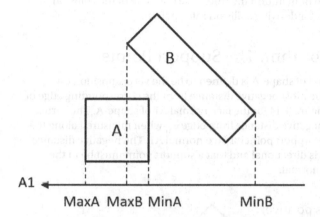

Figure 3-12. *Identify the min and max bound positions for each rectangle*

- **Step 4 Determine overlaps:** Determine if the two min/max bounds overlap. Figure 3-13 shows that the two projected bounds do indeed overlap. In this case, the algorithm cannot conclude and must proceed to process the next face normal. Notice that, as illustrated in the drawing on the right of Figure 3-10, the process of face normal B1 will result in a deterministic conclusion of no collision.

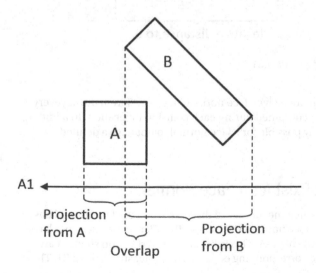

Figure 3-13. *Test for overlap for every axis of projection (example using A1)*

The given algorithm is capable of determining if a collision has occurred with no additional information. Recall that, after detecting a collision, the physics engine must also resolve potential interpenetration and derive a response for the colliding shapes. Both of these computations require additional information—the collision information as introduced in Figure 3-6. The next section introduces an efficient SAT-based algorithm that computes support points to both inform the true/false outcome of the collision detection and serve as the basis for deriving collision information.

An Efficient SAT Algorithm: The Support Points

A support point for a face normal of shape-A is defined to be the vertex position on shape-B where the vertex has the most negative distance from the corresponding edge of shape-A. This is illustrated in Figure 3-14 for the face normal A1 of shape-A. The vertex S_{A1} on shape-B has the largest negative distance from edge e_{A1} when measured along the A1 direction, and thus S_{A1} is the support point for face normal A1. The negative distance signifies that the measurement is directional and that a support point must be in the reverse direction from the face normal.

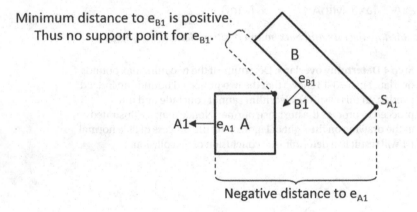

Figure 3-14. Support points of face normals

In general, the support point for a given face normal may be different during every update cycle and thus must be recomputed during each collision invocation. In addition, and very importantly, it is entirely possible for a face normal to not have a defined support point.

Support Point May Not Exist for a Face Normal

A support point is defined only when the measured distance along the face normal has a negative value. For example, the face normal B1 of shape-B in Figure 3-14 does not have a corresponding support point on shape-A. This is because all vertices on shape-A are positive distances away from the corresponding edge e_{B1} when measured along B1. The positive distances signify that all vertices of shape-A are *in front* of the edge e_{B1}. In other words, the entire shape-A is in front of the edge e_{B1} of shape-B and thus the two shapes are not physically touching, and thus they are not colliding.

It follows that, when computing the collision between two shapes, if any of the face normals does not have a corresponding support point, then the two shapes are not colliding. Once again, the early exit capability is an important advantage—the algorithm can return a decision as soon as the first case of undefined support point is detected.

For convenience of discussion and implementation, the distance between a support point and the corresponding edge is referred to as the support point distance and this distance is computed as a positive number. In this way, the support point distance is actually measured along the negative face normal direction. This will be the convention followed in the rest of the discussions in this book.

The Axis of Least Penetration and Collision Information

When support points are defined for all face normals of a convex shape, the face normal of the smallest support point distance is the axis leading to the least interpenetration. Figure 3-15 shows the collision between two shapes where supports points for all of the face normals of shape-B are defined: vertex S_{B1} on shape-A is the corresponding support point for face normal B1, S_{B2} for face normal B2, and so on. In this case, S_{B1} has the smallest corresponding support point distance and thus the face normal B1 is the axis that leads to the least interpenetration. The illustration on the right on Figure 3-15 shows that, in this case, support point distance is the collision depth, face normal B1 is collision normal, support point S_{B1} is the start of the collision, and the end of the collision can be readily computed; it is simply S_{B1} offset by collision depth in the collision normal direction.

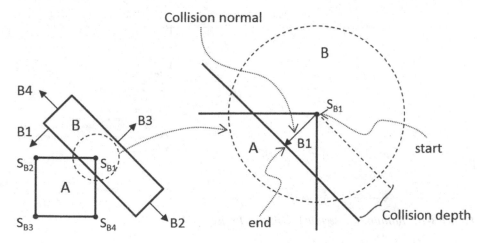

Figure 3-15. *Axis of least penetration and the corresponding collision information*

The Algorithm

With the background description, the efficient SAT-based algorithm to compute the collision between two convex shapes, A and B, can be summarized as:

- Compute the support points for all the face normals on shape-A.

  - If any of the support points is not defined, there is no collision.

  - If all support points are defined, compute the axis of least penetration.

- Compute the support point for all the face normals on shape-B.

  - If any of the support points is not defined, there is no collision.

  - If all support points are defined, compute the axis of least penetration.

The collision information is simply the smaller collision depth from the above two results. You are now ready to implement the support point SAT algorithm.

The Rectangle Collision Project

This project will guide you to implement the support point SAT algorithm. You can see an example of this project running in Figure 3-16. The source code to this project is defined in the Rectangle Collision Project folder.

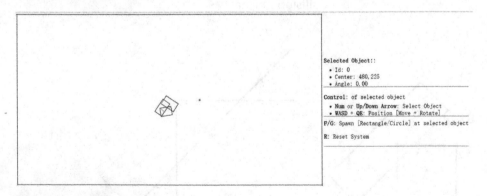

Figure 3-16. Running the Rectangle Collision Project

Project goals:
- To gain insights into and implement the support point SAT algorithm.

Modify Rectangle Collision

Begin by modifying the Rectangle_collision.js file to implement the collision detection between rectangles.

1. Edit the Rectangle_collision.js file in the RigidBody folder.

2. Create a new function findSupportPoint to compute a support point based on dir, the negated face normal direction, and ptOnEdge, a position on the given edge (e.g., a vertex). The following code marches through all the vertices; compute vToEdge, the vector from vertices to ptOnEdge; project this vector onto the input dir, and record the largest positive projected distant. Recall that dir is the negated face normal direction, and thus the largest positive distant corresponds to the furthest vertex position. Additionally, it is entirely possible for all of the projected distances to be negative. In such cases, all vertices are in front of the input dir, a support point does not exist for the given edge, and thus the two rectangles do not collide.

```
Rectangle.prototype.findSupportPoint = function (dir, ptOnEdge) {
    //the longest project length
    var vToEdge;
    var projection;
    // initialize the computed results
    tmpSupport.mSupportPointDist = -9999999;
    tmpSupport.mSupportPoint = null;
    //check each vector of other object
    for (var i = 0; i < this.mVertex.length; i++) {
        vToEdge = this.mVertex[i].subtract(ptOnEdge);
        projection = vToEdge.dot(dir);
        //find the longest distance with certain edge
        //dir is -n direction, so the distance should be positive
        if ((projection > 0) &&
            (projection > tmpSupport.mSupportPointDist)) {
            tmpSupport.mSupportPoint = this.mVertex[i];
            tmpSupport.mSupportPointDist = projection;
        }
    }
};
```

3. With the ability to locate a support point for any face normal, the next step is the find the axis of least penetration by implementing the findAxisLeastPenetration function. Recall that the axis of least penetration is derived based on the support point with the least support point distant. The following code loops over the four face normals, finds the corresponding support point and support point distance, and records the shortest distance. The while-loop signifies that if a support point is not defined for any of the face normals, then the two rectangles do not collide.

```
Rectangle.prototype.findAxisLeastPenetration = function
(otherRect, collisionInfo) {
    var n;
    var supportPoint;
    var bestDistance = 999999;
    var bestIndex = null;
    var hasSupport = true;
    var i = 0;
    while ((hasSupport) && (i < this.mFaceNormal.length)) {
        // Retrieve a face normal from A
        n = this.mFaceNormal[i];
        // use -n as direction and
        // the vectex on edge i as point on edge
        var dir = n.scale(-1);
        var ptOnEdge = this.mVertex[i];
        // find the support on B
        // the point has longest distance with edge i
        otherRect.findSupportPoint(dir, ptOnEdge);
        hasSupport = (tmpSupport.mSupportPoint !== null);
        //get the shortest support point depth
        if ((hasSupport) && (tmpSupport.mSupportPointDist <
        bestDistance)) {
            bestDistance = tmpSupport.mSupportPointDist;
            bestIndex = i;
            supportPoint = tmpSupport.mSupportPoint;
        }
        i = i + 1;
    }
    if (hasSupport) {
        //all four directions have support point
        var bestVec = this.mFaceNormal[bestIndex].
        scale(bestDistance);
        collisionInfo.setInfo(bestDistance, this.
        mFaceNormal[bestIndex], supportPoint.add(bestVec));
    }
    return hasSupport;
};
```

4. You can now implement the collidedRectRect function by computing the axis of least penetration with respect to each of the two rectangles and choosing the smaller of the two results.

```
Rectangle.prototype.collidedRectRect = function (r1, r2,
collisionInfo) {
    var status1 = false;
    var status2 = false;
    //find Axis of Separation for both rectangle
    status1 = r1.findAxisLeastPenetration(r2, collisionInfoR1);
    if (status1) {
        status2 = r2.findAxisLeastPenetration(r1,
        collisionInfoR2);
        if (status2) {
            //choose the shorter normal as the normal
            if (collisionInfoR1.getDepth() < collisionInfoR2.
            getDepth()) {
                var depthVec = collisionInfoR1.getNormal().
                scale(collisionInfoR1.getDepth());
                collisionInfo.setInfo(collisionInfoR1.getDepth(),
                                collisionInfoR1.getNormal(),
                                collisionInfoR1.mStart.
                                subtract(depthVec));
            } else {
                collisionInfo.setInfo(collisionInfoR2.getDepth(),
                                collisionInfoR2.getNormal().
                                scale(-1),
                                collisionInfoR2.mStart);
            }
        }
    }
    return status1 && status2;
};
```

5. Complete the implementation by modifying the collisionTest function to call the newly defined collidedRectRect function to compute the collision between two rectangles.

```
Rectangle.prototype.collisionTest = function (otherShape,
collisionInfo) {
    var status = false;
    if (otherShape.mType === "Circle") {
        status = false;
```

```
            } else {
    status = this.collidedRectRect(this, otherShape,
                                    collisionInfo);
            }
            return status;
        };
```

Observation

You can now run the project to test your implementation. Try creating multiple rectangles with the F key. You can see an orange line representing collision information (collision depth, in the collision normal direction, from start to end) when two or more rectangles collide. Remember that this line shows the least amount of positional correction required to resolve the collision. Use the up and down arrows to select and rotate the rectangles and observe how the collision info changes accordingly. At this stage you have implemented collision detection between a circle and a circle, as well as a rectangle and another rectangle. If you try to collide a rectangle and a circle, no collision info is generated because you have not implemented support for this type of collision. This will be resolved in the next project.

Collision Between Rectangles and Circles

The support point approach to computing collision detection does not work with circles because a circle does not have identifiable vertex positions. Instead, you will implement an algorithm that detects collisions between a rectangle and a circle according to the relative position of the circle's center with respect to the rectangle.

Before discussing the actual algorithm, as illustrated in Figure 3-17, it is convenient to recognize that the area outside an edge of a rectangle can be categorized into three distinct regions by extending the connecting edges. In this case, the dotted lines separated the area outside the given Edge into: R1, the region to the left/top; R2, the region to the right/bottom; and R3, the region immediately outside of the given Edge.

With this background, the collision between a rectangle and a circle can be detected as follows:

- **Step A**: Edge = Compute the nearest edge (the edge on the rectangle that is closest to the circle center).

- **Step B**: If circle center is outside

  - **Step B1**: If in Region R1: the distance between the circle center and left/top vertex from the Edge determines if collision has occurred.

  - **Step B2**: If in Region R2: the distance between the circle center and right/bottom vertex from the Edge determines if collision has occurred.

  - **Step B3**: If in Region R3: the perpendicular distance between the center and the Edge determines if collision has occurred.

- **Step C:** If the circle center is inside the rectangle: collision is detected.

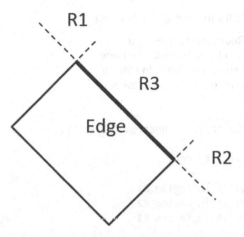

Figure 3-17. *The three regions outside a given edge of a rectangle*

The Rectangle Circle Collision Project

This project guides you in implementing the described rectangle-circle collision detection algorithm with detailed discussions for each of the steps. You can see an example of this project running in Figure 3-18. The source code to this project is defined in the Rectangle Circle Collision Project folder.

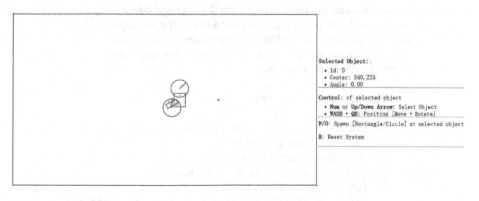

Figure 3-18. *Running the Rectangle Circle Collision Project*

Project goals:

- To understand and implement the rectangle circle collision detection algorithm.

Modify Rectangle Collision

You are going to implement the described algorithm in the Rectangle_collision.js file.

1. Edit the Rectangle_collision.js file in the RigidBody folder.

2. Create a new function, collidedRectCirc, to detect the collision between a rectangle and a circle. Accordingly, there will be five major steps in this function. The following listing collapsed all of the steps with details to be filled in in the rest of this section.

```
Rectangle.prototype.collidedRectCirc = function (otherCir,
collisionInfo) {
    // Step A: Compute the nearest edge
    if (!inside) {
        // Step B1: If center is in Region R1
        // Step B2: If center is in Region R2
        // Step B3: If center is in Region R3
    } else {
        // Step C: If center is inside
    }
    return true;
};
```

3. **Step A**: Compute the nearest edge. The nearest edge can be computed by computing the perpendicular distances between the circle center to each of the edges of the rectangle. This distance is simply the projection of the vector between each vertex and the circle center onto the corresponding face normal. The following code shows marching through all of the vertices, computing the vector from the vertex to the circle center, and projecting the computed vector to the corresponding face normals.

```
// Step A: Compute the nearest edge
for (i = 0; i < 4; ++i) {
    //find the nearest face for center of circle
    circ2Pos = otherCir.mCenter;
    v = circ2Pos.subtract(this.mVertex[i]);
    projection = v.dot(this.mFaceNormal[i]);
    if (projection > 0) {
        //if the center of circle is outside of rectangle
        bestDistance = projection;
        nearestEdge = i;
        inside = false;
        break;
    }
```

```
if (projection > bestDistance) {
    bestDistance = projection;
    nearestEdge = i;
    }
}
```

As illustrated in Figure 3-19, one interesting observation is that when the circle center is inside the rectangle, all vertex-to-center vectors will be in the opposite directions of their corresponding face normal and thus will result in negative projected length. This is in contrast to when the center is outside of the rectangle; then, at least one of the projected lengths is positive. For this reason, the "nearest projected distance" is the one with the least negative value and thus is actually the largest number.

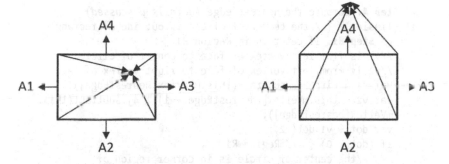

Figure 3-19. *(a) Center inside the rectangle will result in all negative projected length (b) Center outside the rectangle will result in at least one positive projected length*

4. **Step B1**: if center is outside of the rectangle and in Region R1. As illustrated in Figure 3-20-a, the Region R1 can be detected when $\vec{V}_1$, the vector between the center and the edge vertex, is in the opposite direction of $\vec{V}_2$, the direction of the edge. This is to say, the center of the circle is in Region R1 when the dot product of those two vectors is negative. Figure 3-20-b shows that collision occurs when the length of vector $\vec{V}_1$ is less than the circle radius, and in this case, the collision normal is simply along the vector $\vec{V}_1$, and collision depth is the difference between the radius and dist, the length of vector $\vec{V}_1$

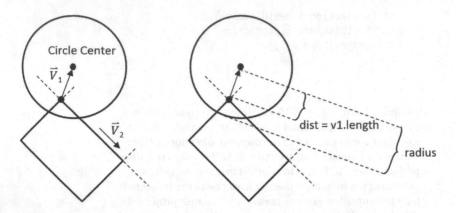

Figure 3-20. *(a) Condition when center is in Region R1 (b) The corresponding collision information*

```
// Step A: Compute the nearest edge (details discussed)
if (!inside) { //the center of circle is outside of rectangle
    // Step B1: if ceter is in Region R1
    //v1 is from left vertex of face to center of circle
    //v2 is from left vertex of face to right vertex of face
    var v1 = circ2Pos.subtract(this.mVertex[nearestEdge]);
    var v2 = this.mVertex[(nearestEdge + 1) % 4].subtract(this.
    mVertex[nearestEdge]);
    var dot = v1.dot(v2);
    if (dot < 0) {   // Region R1
        //the center of circle is in corner region of
        mVertex[nearestEdge]
        var dis = v1.length();
        //compare the distance with radium to decide collision
        if (dis > otherCir.mRadius)
            return false;
        var normal = v1.normalize();
        var radiusVec = normal.scale(-otherCir.mRadius);
        collisionInfo.setInfo(otherCir.mRadius - dis, normal,
                            circ2Pos.add(radiusVec));
    } else {   // Not in Region R1
        // ... details to follow ...
        // Step B2: If center is in Region B2
        if (...) { // in Region R2
            // ... details to follow ...
        } else {   // not in Region R2
            // Step B3: If center is in Region B3
            // ... details to follow ...
        }
    }
}
```

```
} else {   // else of (!inside)
    // Step C: If center is inside the rectangle
    // ... details to follow ...
}
```

5. **Step B2**: if the center is outside of the rectangle and in Region R2. The following code complements that of Step B1, with the only difference being the direction of $\vec{V}_2$, the vector along the edge. In this case, the vector along the edge is in the opposite direction as compared to working with Region R1.

```
// Step A: Compute the nearest edge (details discussed)
if (!inside) {
    // Step B1: If center is in Region R1 (detailed discussed)
} else {
    // Step B2: If center is in Region R2
    //the center of circle is in corner region of
    mVertex[nearestEdge+1]
    //v1 is from right vertex of face to center of circle
    //v2 is from right vertex of face to left vertex of face
    var v1 = circ2Pos.subtract(this.mVertex[(nearestEdge + 1) % 4]);
    var v2 = v2.scale(-1);
    var dot = v1.dot(v2);
    if (dot < 0) {
        var dis = v1.length();
        //compare the distance with radium to decide collision
        if (dis > otherCir.mRadius)
            return false;
        var normal = v1.normalize();
        var radiusVec = normal.scale(-otherCir.mRadius);
        collisionInfo.setInfo(otherCir.mRadius - dis, normal,
        circ2Pos.add(radiusVec));
    } else {
        // Step B3: If center is in Region B3
        // ... details to follow ...
    }
}
```

6. **Step B3**: If the center is in Region R3. The last possible region for the circle center to be located in would be the area immediately outside the nearest edge. In this case, the bestDistance computed previously in **Step A** is the distance; if this distance is less than the circle radius, then collision occurred.

```
// Step B3: If center is in Region B3
//the center of circle is in face region of face[nearestEdge]
```

```
        if (bestDistance < otherCir.mRadius) {
            var radiusVec = this.mFaceNormal[nearestEdge].scale(otherCir.
            mRadius);
            collisionInfo.setInfo(otherCir.mRadius - bestDistance,
                            this.mFaceNormal[nearestEdge], circ2Pos.
                            subtract(radiusVec));
        } else {
            return false;
        }
```

7. **Step C**: If the circle center is inside the rectangle, then collision is detected and the corresponding collision information can be computed and returned.

```
            if (!inside) {
                //... conditions for Region R1, R2, and R3 as
                discussed
            } else {
                //the center of circle is inside of rectangle
                var radiusVec = this.mFaceNormal[nearestEdge].
                scale(otherCir.mRadius);
                collisionInfo.setInfo
                    (otherCir.mRadius - bestDistance,
                    this.mFaceNormal[nearestEdge],
                    circ2Pos.subtract(radiusVec));
            }
            return true;
        };
```

8. The last step is to modify the `collisionTest` function to call the newly defined collision function accordingly.

```
    Rectangle.prototype.collisionTest = function (otherShape,
    collisionInfo) {
        var status = false;
        if (otherShape.mType === "Circle") {
            status = this.collidedRectCirc(otherShape,
            collisionInfo);
        } else {
            status = this.collidedRectRect(this, otherShape,
            collisionInfo);
        }
        return status;
    };
```

Observation

You can now run the project to test your implementation. You can create rectangles and circles, move and rotate them to observe the corresponding collision information represented by orange lines. Rotate colliding rectangles to observe the collision information, adapting to the shape's rotation. That is because the calculated collision information is dependent on the position of the vertex and face normal of the rectangle. However, when you rotate a colliding circle, the collision information does not change. That is because the calculated collision information is only dependent on the circle's center position and its radius. For this reason, the rotation of a circle does not change its collision information.

Summary

At this stage, your physics engine simulation is capable of detecting collisions accurately, and computing the appropriate collision information when rigid shapes collide. You have been introduced to broad phase method, the Separating Axis Theorem, and support points for efficiently detecting collisions of convex shapes. You have implemented algorithms based on these concepts that successfully detect collisions and compute the associated information necessary for resolving any potential interpenetrations. The next chapter will introduce you to some elementary physics about movements, and how to use the computed collision information for simulating a real-world physics interaction in 2D space by properly resolving collisions.

CHAPTER 4

■ ■ ■

Completing the Physics Engine and Rigid Shape Component

In the previous chapter, you have implemented algorithms to detect collisions between rigid circles and rectangles. In addition to the boolean condition of whether a collision has indeed occurred, the algorithms you have implemented also computed information that tells you important details—the collision information, which includes the interpenetration depth and normal direction. In this chapter, you will further expand the physics engine by using the collision information to correct the interpenetration condition, and learn about simulating collision responses that resemble real-world rigid shape behaviors. Initially, your responses will be in linear motion, and finally you will support objects rotating as a result of collisions.

To begin with this last phase of the investigation, you will first amend the rigid shape classes to support proper simulation of Newtonian motion and to include relevant physical attributes to allow the simulation of energy transfers between colliding objects. After you implement movements in the physics engine together with the collision detection algorithms from the previous chapter, you can start resolving collisions. Collisions are resolved by correcting the interpenetration state of the rigid shapes, and instituting a proper response. Interpenetrations will be corrected by moving the colliding shapes apart such that they do not overlap, and collision responses will be instituted based on the Impulse Method to simulate the transfer of both linear and angular momentum.

After completing this chapter, you will be able to:

- Understand how to approximate integrals with Euler Method and Symplectic Euler Integration.

- Approximate Newtonian motion formulation with Symplectic Euler Integration.

- Resolve interpenetrating collisions based on a numerically stable relaxation method.

© Michael Tanaya, Huaming Chen, Jebediah Pavleas and Kelvin Sung 2017
M. Tanaya et al., *Building a 2D Game Physics Engine*, DOI 10.1007/978-1-4842-2583-7_4

- Compute and implement responses to collisions that resemble the responses of rigid bodies in the real-world.

- Complete the physics engine in simulating the collisions and responses of rigid circles and rectangles.

Movement

Movement is the description of how object positions change in the simulated world. Mathematically, movement can be formulated in many ways. In previous chapters, you experienced working with movement where you continuously changed the position of an object with a constant value, or a displacement. Although desired results can be achieved, mathematically this is problematic because a velocity and a position are different types of quantities with different units and the two cannot be simply combined. As illustrated in Figure 4-1 and the following equation, in practice, you have been working with describing movement based on constant displacements.

- $p_{new} = p_{current} + displacement$

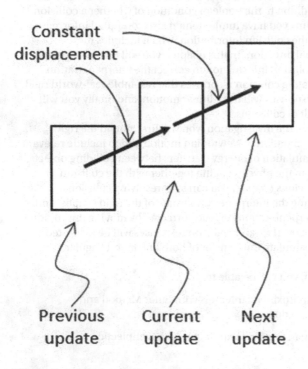

Figure 4-1. Movement Based on Constant Displacements

A movement that is governed by the constant displacement formulation becomes restrictive when it is necessary to change the amount that is displaced over time. Newtonian mechanics address this restriction by considering time in the movement formulations, as seen in the following equations.

- $v_{new} = v_{current} + \int a(t)dt$

- $p_{new} = p_{current} + \int v(t)dt$

These two equations implement a Newtonian based movement where $v(t)$ is the velocity that describes the change in position over time and $a(t)$ is the acceleration that describes the change in velocity over time.

Notice that both velocity and acceleration are vector quantities encoding the change in magnitude and direction. The magnitude of a velocity vector defines the speed, and the normalized velocity vector identifies the direction that the object is traveling. An acceleration vector lets you know whether an object is speeding up or slowing down via its magnitude and the direction that the acceleration is occurring in. Acceleration is changed by the forces acting upon an object. For example, if you were to throw a ball into the air, the gravitational force of the earth would affect the object's acceleration over time, which in turn would change the object's velocity.

Explicit Euler Integration

The following two equations show that the Euler method, or Explicit Euler Integration, approximates integrals based on initial values. Though potentially unstable, this is one of the simplest and thus a good beginning point to learn about integration approximation methods. As illustrated in the following two equations, in the case of the Newtonian movement formulation the new velocity, v_{new}, of the object can be approximated as the current velocity, $v_{current}$, plus the current acceleration, $a_{current}$, multiplied by the amount of elapsed time. Similarly, the object's new position, p_{new}, can be approximated by the object's current position, $p_{current}$, plus the current velocity, $v_{current}$, multiplied by the amount of elapsed time.

■ **Note**   An example of a numerically unstable system is one where under gravitational force a bouncing ball slows down but never stops jittering and, in some cases, may even start bouncing again.

- $v_{new} = v_{current} + a_{current} * dt$

- $p_{new} = p_{current} + v_{current} * dt$

The left diagram of Figure 4-2 illustrates a simple example of approximating movements with Explicit Euler Integration. Notice that the new position p_{new} is computed based on the current velocity, $v_{current}$, while the new velocity v_{new}, is computed to move the position for the next update cycle.

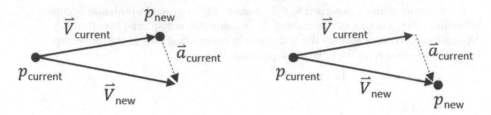

Figure 4-2. *Explicit (Left) and Symplectic (Right) Euler Integration*

Symplectic Euler Integration

In practice, because of system stability concerns, Explicit Euler Integration is seldom implemented. This shortcoming is overcome with the method you will be implementing, known as the Semi-Implicit Euler Integration or Symplectic Euler Integration, where intermediate results are used in subsequent approximations. The following equations show Symplectic Euler Integration. Notice that it is nearly identical to the Euler method except that the new velocity, v_{new}, is being used when calculating the new position, p_{new}. This essentially means that the velocity for the next frame is being used to calculate the position of this frame.

- $v_{new} = v_{current} + a_{current} * dt$

- $p_{new} = p_{current} + v_{new} * dt$

The right diagram of Figure 4-2 illustrates that with the Symplectic Euler Integration, the new position p_{new} is computed based on the newly computed velocity, v_{new}.

Implementing Symplectic Euler Integration and Defining Attributes to Support Collision Response

You are now ready to implement Symplectic Euler Integration. The fixed time step update function architecture of the game engine allows the *dt* quantity to be implemented as the update time interval and the integral to be evaluated once per update cycle.

In addition to implement Symplectic Euler Integration, this project also defines the attributes and their corresponding accessor and getter functions. Though relatively straightforward, these functions are presented here to avoid distracting the discussions of the more complex concepts to be covered in the subsequent projects.

You will modify the `RigidShape` class for this implementation.

The Rigid Shape Movement Project

This project will guide you through completing the rigid shape component to support movement calculations and collision responses. In addition to implement Symplectic Euler Integration, the information that you are going to add includes the attributes required for collision simulation and response, such as mass, inertia, friction, and restitution. As will be explained, each of these attributes will play a part in the calculation of simulating object movements and collision responses based on Euler integration. You can see an example of this project running in Figure 4-3. The source code to this project is defined in the Rigid Shape Movements Project folder.

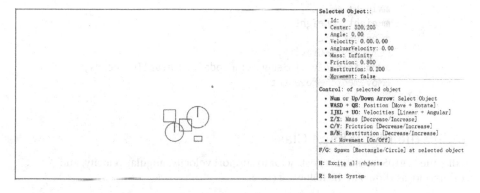

Figure 4-3. *Running the Rigid Shape Movements Project*

Project Goals:

- To experience implementing movements based on Symplectic Euler Integration.

- To complete the implementation of RigidShape classes to include relevant physical attributes.

- To build the infrastructure for responding to collisions.

Implement Symplectic Euler Integration

You must define movement support and constants in the core of the engine and in rigid shape.

Modify the Engine Core

Let's start with the engine core:

1. Modify the Core.js file to include two more instance variables in the constructor, the first to support applying gravity on all objects, and the second to enable/disable object movements.

```
var mGravity = new Vec2(0, 10);
var mMovement = false;
```

2. Update the mPublic variable to allow external access to the newly defined instances.

```
var mPublic = {
    initializeEngineCore: initializeEngineCore,
    mAllObject: mAllObject,
    mWidth: mWidth,
    mHeight: mHeight,
    mContext: mContext,
    mGravity: mGravity,
    mUpdateIntervalInSeconds: mUpdateIntervalInSeconds,
    mMovement: mMovement
};
```

Modify the RigidShape Class

Modify the RigidShape class constructor to support velocity, angular velocity, and acceleration, as shown in the following code.

```
function RigidShape(center, mass, friction, restitution) {
    this.mCenter = center;
    this.mVelocity = new Vec2(0, 0);
    this.mAcceleration = gEngine.Core.mGravity;

    //angle
    this.mAngle = 0;
    //negetive-- clockwise
    //positive-- counterclockwise
    this.mAngularVelocity = 0;

    this.mAngularAcceleration = 0;

    gEngine.Core.mAllObject.push(this);
}
```

Implement Symplectic Euler Integration

You can now add the behavior to the rigid shape object for numerical integration. Continue with the RigidShape base class, and complete the update function to apply Symplectic Euler Integration to the rigid shape where the updated velocity is used for computing the new position. Notice the implementation similarities between linear and angular motion. In both cases, the velocities are updated before the results are being applied to the displacements. Rotation will be examined in detail in the last section of this chapter.

```
RigidShape.prototype.update = function () {
    if (gEngine.Core.mMovement) {
        var dt = gEngine.Core.mUpdateIntervalInSeconds;
        //v += a*t
        this.mVelocity = this.mVelocity.add(this.mAcceleration.scale(dt));
        //s += v*t
        this.move(this.mVelocity.scale(dt));

        this.mAngularVelocity += this.mAngularAcceleration * dt;
        this.rotate(this.mAngularVelocity * dt);
    }
};
```

Define Attributes to Support Collision Simulation and Response

As mentioned, in order to allow focused discussions of the more complex concepts in the later sections, the attributes for supporting collisions and the corresponding supporting functions are introduced in this project. These attributes are defined in the RigidShape class.

Modify the RigidShape Class

Now it's time for the RigidShape class:

1. Modify the RigidShape class constructor again, this time to support mass, restitution (bounciness), and friction, as shown in the following code. Notice that the inverse of the mass value is actually stored for computation efficiency (by avoiding an extra division during each update calculation). Additionally, notice that a mass of zero is used to represent a stationary object.

    ```
    function RigidShape(center, mass, friction, restitution) {
        this.mCenter = center;
        this.mInertia = 0;
        if (mass !== undefined)
            this.mInvMass = mass;
        else
            this.mInvMass = 1;

        if (friction !== undefined)
            this.mFriction = friction;
        else
            this.mFriction = 0.8;

        if (restitution !== undefined)
            this.mRestitution = restitution;
        else
    ```

```
        this.mRestitution = 0.2;

    this.mVelocity = new Vec2(0, 0);

    if (this.mInvMass !== 0) {
        this.mInvMass = 1 / this.mInvMass;
        this.mAcceleration = gEngine.Core.mGravity;
    } else {
        this.mAcceleration = new Vec2(0, 0);
    }

    //angle
    this.mAngle = 0;
    //negetive-- clockwise
    //positive-- counterclockwise
    this.mAngularVelocity = 0;

    this.mAngularAcceleration = 0;

    this.mBoundRadius = 0;

    gEngine.Core.mAllObject.push(this);
}
```

2. Define a function, updateMass, to support changing of
    the mass during runtime. Notice that the updateInertia
    function is empty. This reflects the fact that rotational inertia
    is shape-specific and the actual implementation would be the
    responsibility of individual subclasses (Rectangle and Circle).

```
RigidShape.prototype.updateMass = function (delta) {
    var mass;
    if (this.mInvMass !== 0)
        mass = 1 / this.mInvMass;
    else
        mass = 0;

    mass += delta;
    if (mass <= 0) {
        this.mInvMass = 0;
        this.mVelocity = new Vec2(0, 0);
        this.mAcceleration = new Vec2(0, 0);
        this.mAngularVelocity = 0;
        this.mAngularAcceleration = 0;
    } else {
        this.mInvMass = 1 / mass;
        this.mAcceleration = gEngine.Core.mGravity;
```

```
        }
        this.updateInertia();
    };


    RigidShape.prototype.updateInertia = function () {
        // subclass must define this.
        // must work with inverted this.mInvMass
    };
```

Modify the Circle and Rectangle Classes

Next, modify the Circle and Rectangle classes:

1. Modify the Circle class to implement the updateInertia
    function. This function calculates the rotational inertia of a
    circle when its mass is changed.

    ```
    Circle.prototype.updateInertia = function() {
        if (this.mInvMass === 0) {
            this.mInertia = 0;
        } else {
            // this.mInvMass is inverted!!
            // Inertia-mass * radius^2
            // 12 is a constant value that can be changed
            this.mInertia = (1 / this.mInvMass) * (this.mRadius *
            this.mRadius) / 12;
        }
    };
    ```

2. Update the Circle object constructor to call the new
    RigidShape base class, and to accept relevant parameters
    of physical attributes. Remember to call the newly defined
    updateInertia for initialization.

    ```
    var Circle = function (center, radius, mass, friction,
    restitution) {
        RigidShape.call(this, center, mass, friction, restitution);
        this.mType = "Circle";
        //...identical to previous project
        this.updateInertia();
    };
    ```

3. Modify the Rectangle class to implement its updateIntertia
    function.

    ```
    Rectangle.prototype.updateInertia = function() {
    ```

```
        // Expect this.mInvMass to be already inverted!
        if (this.mInvMass === 0)
            this.mInertia = 0;
        else {
            //inertia=mass*width^2+height^2
            this.mInertia = (1 / this.mInvMass) * (this.mWidth *
            this.mWidth + this.mHeight * this.mHeight) / 12;
            this.mInertia = 1 / this.mInertia;
        }
    };
```

4. Update the Rectangle constructor in a similar manner to the
    Circle class to accept the relevant parameters of physical
    attributes and to invoke the newly defined shape-specific
    updateIntertia function.

```
    var Rectangle = function (center, width, height, mass, friction,
    restitution) {
        RigidShape.call(this, center, mass, friction, restitution);
        this.mType = "Rectangle";
        this.mWidth = width;
        this.mHeight = height;
        //...indetical to previous project
        this.updateInertia();
    };
```

Modify the updateUIEcho Function

Since the engine has become more powerful and flexible, you want the UI to display the
corresponding attributes and allow the user to control these for testing purposes. Modify
the updateUIEcho function in the Core.js file to print out all the options of user control.

```
var updateUIEcho = function () {
    document.getElementById("uiEchoString").innerHTML =
        "<p><b>Selected Object:</b>:</p>" +
        "<ul style=\"margin:-10px\">" +
        "<li>Id: " + gObjectNum + "</li>" +
        "<li>Center: " + mAllObject[gObjectNum].mCenter.x.toPrecision(3) +
        "," + mAllObject[gObjectNum].mCenter.y.toPrecision(3) + "</li>" +
        "<li>Angle: " + mAllObject[gObjectNum].mAngle.toPrecision(3) + "</li>" +
        "<li>Velocity: " + mAllObject[gObjectNum].mVelocity.x.toPrecision(3) +
        "," + mAllObject[gObjectNum].mVelocity.y.toPrecision(3) + "</li>" +
        "<li>AngluarVelocity: " + mAllObject[gObjectNum].mAngularVelocity.
        toPrecision(3) + "</li>" +
        "<li>Mass: " + 1 / mAllObject[gObjectNum].mInvMass.toPrecision(3) +
        "</li>" +
```

```
        "<li>Friction: " + mAllObject[gObjectNum].mFriction.toPrecision(3) +
        "</li>" +
        "<li>Restitution: " + mAllObject[gObjectNum].mRestitution.
        toPrecision(3) + "</li>" +
        "<li>Movement: " + gEngine.Core.mMovement + "</li>" +
        "</ul> <hr>" +
        "<p><b>Control</b>: of selected object</p>" +
        "<ul style=\"margin:-10px\">" +
        "<li><b>Num</b> or <b>Up/Down Arrow</b>: Select Object</li>" +
        "<li><b>WASD</b> + <b>QE</b>: Position [Move + Rotate]</li>" +
        "<li><b>IJKL</b> + <b>UO</b>: Velocities [Linear + Angular]</li>" +
        "<li><b>Z/X</b>: Mass [Decrease/Increase]</li>" +
        "<li><b>C/V</b>: Frictrion [Decrease/Increase]</li>" +
        "<li><b>B/N</b>: Restitution [Decrease/Increase]</li>" +
        "<li><b>,</b>: Movement [On/Off]</li>" +
        "</ul> <hr>" +
        "<b>F/G</b>: Spawn [Rectangle/Circle] at selected object" +
        "<p><b>H</b>: Excite all objects</p>" +
        "<p><b>R</b>: Reset System</p>" +
        "<hr>";
};
```

Modify the userControl function

For testing purposes, you want to update the UserControl.js file to allow the
modification of game engine attributes during runtime. Add the following cases to the
userControl function.

```
//... identical to previous project
if (keycode === 73)       //I
    gEngine.Core.mAllObject[gObjectNum].mVelocity.y -= 1;
if (keycode === 75)       //k
    gEngine.Core.mAllObject[gObjectNum].mVelocity.y += 1;
if (keycode === 74)       //j
    gEngine.Core.mAllObject[gObjectNum].mVelocity.x -= 1;
if (keycode === 76)       //l
    gEngine.Core.mAllObject[gObjectNum].mVelocity.x += 1;
if (keycode === 85)       //U
    gEngine.Core.mAllObject[gObjectNum].mAngularVelocity -= 0.1;
if (keycode === 79)       //O
    gEngine.Core.mAllObject[gObjectNum].mAngularVelocity += 0.1;
if (keycode === 90)       //Z
    gEngine.Core.mAllObject[gObjectNum].updateMass(-1);
if (keycode === 88)       //X
    gEngine.Core.mAllObject[gObjectNum].updateMass(1);
if (keycode === 67)       //C
    gEngine.Core.mAllObject[gObjectNum].mFriction -= 0.01;
```

```
if (keycode === 86)      //V
    gEngine.Core.mAllObject[gObjectNum].mFriction += 0.01;
if (keycode === 66)      //B
    gEngine.Core.mAllObject[gObjectNum].mRestitution -= 0.01;
if (keycode === 78)      //N
    gEngine.Core.mAllObject[gObjectNum].mRestitution += 0.01;
if (keycode === 188)     //'
    gEngine.Core.mMovement = !gEngine.Core.mMovement;
if (keycode === 70)      //f
    var r1 = new Rectangle(new Vec2(gEngine.Core.mAllObjects[gObjectNum].mCenter.x,
                            gEngine.Core.mAllObjects[gObjectNum].mCenter.y),
                Math.random() * 30 + 10, Math.random() * 30 + 10,
                Math.random() * 30, Math.random(), Math.random());
if (keycode === 71)      //g
    var r1 = new Circle(new Vec2(gEngine.Core.mAllObjects[gObjectNum].mCenter.x,
                            gEngine.Core.mAllObjects[gObjectNum].mCenter.y),
                Math.random() * 10 + 20, Math.random() * 30,
                Math.random(), Math.random());
if (keycode === 72) {    //H
    var i;
    for (i = 0; i < gEngine.Core.mAllObject.length; i++) {
        if (gEngine.Core.mAllObject[i].mInvMass !== 0)
            gEngine.Core.mAllObject[i].mVelocity =
                new Vec2(Math.random() * 20 - 10, Math.random() * 20 - 10);
    }
}
//... identical to previous project
```

Observation

Run the project to test your implementation. Create a few objects in the scene; you can examine the attributes of your selected object. Notice that when you enable the movement by pressing the comma (,) key, the objects with higher downward initial velocity will drop faster because of the gravitational force or acceleration. Now create an object and set its initial y-velocity to negative. Observe that the object will move upwards until the y-component velocity reaches zero, and then it will start to fall downwards as a result of gravitational acceleration. You can also change the object's initial x-velocity and observe the motion of a projectile. Another interesting case to try is to create a few objects and excite them by pressing the H key. Observe how all the objects move according to their own velocities. You may see objects that move beyond the scene boundary. This is because at this point the physics engine does not support collision resolution. This will be remedied in the next section.

Resolving Interpenetrations

In the context of game engines, collision resolution refers to the process that determines how objects respond after a collision, including strategies to resolve the potential interpenetration situations that may occur. Notice that there are no collision resolution processes in the real world where interpenetration of rigid objects cannot occur since collisions are strictly governed by the law of physics. Resolutions of interpenetrations are relevant only in a virtual simulated world, where movements are approximated and impossible conditions may occur but can be resolved in ways that are desirable to the developer or designer.

In general, there are three common methods for responding to interpenetrating collisions. The first is to simply displace the objects from one another by the depth of penetration. This is known as the Projection Method since you simply move an object's position so that it no longer penetrates the other. While this is simple to calculate and implement, it lacks stability when many objects are in proximity and resting upon one another. The simple resolving of one pair of interpenetrating objects can result in new penetrations with other nearby objects. However, this is still a common method for simple engines or games with simple object interaction rules. For example, in the Pong game, the ball never comes to rest on the paddles or walls and continuously remains in motion by bouncing off any object it collides with. The Projection Method is perfect for resolving collisions for these types of simple object interactions. The second method is known as the Impulse Method, which uses object velocities to compute and apply impulses to initiate the objects to move in the opposite directions at the point of collision. This method tends to slow down colliding objects rapidly and converges to relatively stable solutions. This is because impulses are computed based on the transfer of momentum, which in turn has a damping effect on the velocities of the colliding objects. The third method is known as the Penalty Method, which models the depth of object interpenetration as the degree of compression of a spring and approximates an acceleration to apply forces to separate the objects. This last method is the most complex and challenging to implement.

For your engine, you will be combining the strengths of the Projection and Impulse Methods. The Projection Method will be used to separate the interpenetrating objects, while the Impulse Method will be used to apply small impulses to reduce the object velocities in the direction that caused the interpenetration. As described, the simple Projection Method can result in an unstable system, such as objects that sink into each other when stacked. You will overcome this instability by implementing a relaxation loop where interpenetrated objects are separated incrementally via repeated applications of the Projection Method in a single update cycle. With a relaxation loop, the number of times that the Projection Method is applied is referred to as the *relaxation iterations*. During each relaxation iteration, the Projection Method reduces the interpenetration incrementally by a fixed percentage of the total penetration depth. For example, by default the engine sets relaxation iterations to 15, and during each relaxation iteration the interpenetration is reduced by 80%. This means that within one update function call, after the movement integration approximation, the collision detection and resolution procedures will be executed 15 times. While costly, the repeated incremental separation ensures a stable system under normal circumstances. However, the 15 relaxation iterations may not be sufficient when the system undergoes sudden large changes. For example, if a large number of significantly overlapped objects, e.g., 100 overlapped circles, were to be added to the system simultaneously, then the 15 relaxation iterations may not be sufficient. This situation can be resolved by increasing the relaxation iterations at the cost of a loss in performance. From our experience, under normal operation conditions, a relaxation iteration of around 15 is a balanced trade-off between accuracy and performance.

The Positional Correction Project

This project will guide you through the implementation of the relaxation iterations to incrementally resolve inter-object interpenetrations. You are going to use the collision information computed from the previous chapter to correct the position of the colliding objects. You can see an example of this project running in Figure 4-4. The source code to this project is defined in the Positional Correction Project folder.

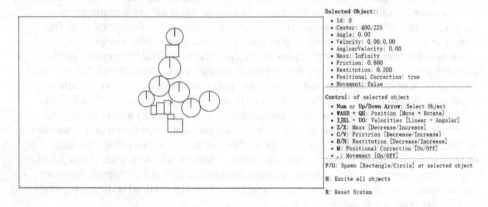

Figure 4-4. Running the Positional Correction Project

Project Goals:

- To appreciate the importance of the computed collision information.

- To implement positional correction with relaxation iteration.

- To understand and experience implementing interpenetration resolution.

Update the Physics Engine

This project will only modify Physics.js because this is the file that implements the details of collisions.

1. Edit Physics.js and add in the following variables to support the correction of positions incrementally via the relaxation iterations.

```
//...identical to previous project
gEngine.Physics = (function () {
    var mPositionalCorrectionFlag = true;
    // number of relaxation iteration
    var mRelaxationCount = 15;
    // percentage of separation to project objects
    var mPosCorrectionRate = 0.8;

    //... identical to previous project

    var mPublic = {
        collision: collision,
        mPositionalCorrectionFlag: mPositionalCorrectionFlag
    };
    return mPublic;
}());
```

2. Modify the collision function to include an enclosing relaxation iteration loop over the collision detection loop.

```
var collision = function () {
    var i, j, k;
    for (k = 0; k < mRelaxationCount; k++) {
        for (i = 0; i < gEngine.Core.mAllObject.length; i++) {
            //...identical to previous project
        }
    }
};
```

3. Create a new function in gEngine.Physics and name
   it positionalCorrection. This function reduces the
   overlaps between objects by the predefined constant
   mPosCorrectionRate with a default value of 80%. To properly
   support object momentum in the simulation, the amount in
   which each object moves is governed by their corresponding
   masses. For example, upon the collision of two objects, the
   object with a larger mass will generally move by an amount
   that is less than the object with smaller mass. Notice that
   the direction of movement is along the collision normal as
   defined in the collisionInfo structure.

```
var positionalCorrection = function (s1, s2, collisionInfo) {
    var s1InvMass = s1.mInvMass;
    var s2InvMass = s2.mInvMass;

    var num = collisionInfo.getDepth() /
            (s1InvMass + s2InvMass) * mPosCorrectionRate;
    var correctionAmount = collisionInfo.getNormal().scale(num);

    s1.move(correctionAmount.scale(-s1InvMass));
    s2.move(correctionAmount.scale(s2InvMass));
};
```

4. Create another function and name it resolveCollision. This
   function receives two RigidShape objects as parameter, and
   determines if the collision detected should be positionally
   corrected. As pointed out previously, objects with infinite
   mass, or zero inversed mass, are stationary and will not
   participate in positional correction after a collision.

```
var resolveCollision = function (s1, s2, collisionInfo) {
    if ((s1.mInvMass === 0) && (s2.mInvMass === 0))
        return;
    // correct positions
    if(gEngine.Physics.mPositionalCorrectionFlag)
        positionalCorrection(s1, s2, collisionInfo);
};
```

5. Finally, you should call the newly defined resolveCollision
   function from within the collision function when a collision
   is detected. You can invoke resolveCollision after calling
   the drawCollisionInfo function.

```
var collision = function () {
    var i, j, k;
    var collisionInfo = new CollisionInfo();
    for (k = 0; k < mRelaxationCount; k++) {
        //....identical to previous project
        drawCollisionInfo(collisionInfo, gEngine.Core.mContext);
        resolveCollision(gEngine.Core.mAllObject[i],
                         gEngine.Core.mAllObject[j],
                         collisionInfo);
        //... identical to previous project
```

Note that the drawCollisionInfo function is a drawing operation and, strictly speaking, does not belong within the update loop in the collision function. Additionally, this draw operation is invoked within the core of relaxation loop iterations, which is computationally expensive. Fortunately, this function is for debugging purposes and will be commented out after this project.

Observation

Run the project to test your implementation. Create a few objects in the scene. Notice that with the M key, you can control whether the newly created objects overlap. Now, reset the scene with the R key, and then create some objects followed by enabling movement. You will notice small amounts of interpenetration happening and, when left alone, objects may begin to sink below the bottom of the scene. Select any of the objects to notice the ever-increasing negative y-velocity component. During each update cycle, all objects' y-velocities are changed by gravitational acceleration, and yet the positional correction relaxation iterations are preventing them from moving downwards. By disabling the movement, you will notice overlaps disappearing completely, as positional correction will not be countered anymore. The ever-increasing y-velocities of the objects are a serious concern when attempting to create a stable system. Continuously increasing/decreasing numbers will result in unstable and unpredictable behavior, as witnessed in the objects sinking below the bottom boundary. In the following sections you will learn about the Impulse Method to further improve collision resolutions.

Resolving Collisions

With a functioning positional correction system, you can now begin implementing collision resolution and support behaviors that resemble real-world situations. In order to focus on the core functionality of a collision resolution system, including understanding and implementing the Impulse Method and ensuring system stability, you will continue to work with axis-aligned rigid shapes. The complications associated with angular impulse resolutions will be examined in the next section, after the mechanics behind linear impulse resolution are fully understood and implemented.

In the following discussion, the rectangles and circles will not rotate as a response to collisions. However, the concepts and implementation described generalize to support rotational collision responses. This project is designed to help you understand the basic concepts of impulse-based collision resolution with axis-aligned shapes.

Formulating the Impulse Method

You will formulate the solution for the Impulse Method by first reviewing how a circle can bounce off of a wall and other circles in a perfect world. This will subsequently be used to derive an approximation for an appropriate collision response. Note that the following discussion focuses on deriving the formulation for the Impulse Method and does not attempt to present a review on the fundamentals of Newtonian Mechanics. Here is a brief review of some of the relevant terms.

- Mass is the amount of matter in an object, or how dense an object is.

- Force is any interaction or energy imparted on an object that will change the motion of that object.

- Relative Velocity is the difference in velocity between two travelling shapes.

- Coefficient of Restitution is the ratio of relative velocity after and before a collision. This is a measure of how much of the kinetic energy remains for the object to rebound from one another, or bounciness.

- Coefficient of Friction is a number that describes the ratio of the force of friction between two bodies. In your very simplistic implementation, friction is applied directly to slow down linear motion or rotation.

- Impulse is accumulated force over time that can cause a change in the velocity, for example, resulting from a collision.

Decomposing the Velocity in a Collision

Figure 4-5 illustrates a circle A in three different stages. At stage 1 the circle is traveling at velocity $\vec{V}_1$ towards the wall on its right. At stage 2 the circle is colliding with the wall. At stage 3 the circle has been reflected and is traveling away from the wall with velocity $\vec{V}_2$.

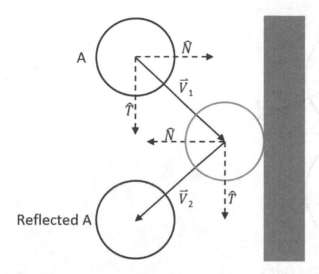

Figure 4-5. *Collision Between a Circle and a Wall in a Perfect World*

Mathematically, this collision and its response can be described by decomposing the initial velocity, $\vec{V}_1$, into the components that are parallel, or tangent T, and perpendicular, or normal $\hat{N}$, to the colliding wall. As seen in the following equation,

- $V_1 = (\vec{V}_1 \cdot \hat{N})\hat{N} + (\vec{V}_1 \cdot \hat{T})\hat{T}$

In a perfect world with no friction and no loss of kinetic energy, after the collision, the component along the tangent direction will not be affect while the normal component will be simply reversed. In this way, the reflected vector $\vec{V}_2$ can be expressed as a linear combination of normal and tangent components of $\vec{V}_1$ as followed.

- $\vec{V}_2 = -(\vec{V}_1 \cdot \hat{N})\hat{N} + (\vec{V}_1 \cdot \hat{T})\hat{T}$

Notice the negative sign in front of the $\hat{N}$ component. You can see in Figure 4-5, that the $\hat{N}$ component for vector $\vec{V}_2$ points in the opposite direction of that of $\vec{V}_1$ as a result of the collision. Notice also that the tangent component, $\hat{T}$, is still pointing in the same direction since it is parallel to the of the wall and is unaffected by the collision. This demonstrates a vector reflection.

Relative Velocity of Colliding Shapes

This decomposition of vectors into the normal and tangent directions of the collision also applies in the general cases when the colliding shapes are both in motion. For example Figure 4-6 illustrates two traveling circle shapes, A and B, colliding.

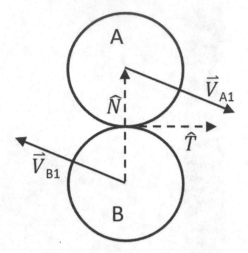

Figure 4-6. *Collision Between Two Circles*

In the case of Figure 4-6, before the collision, shape A is traveling with velocity $\vec{V}_{A1}$ while shape B with velocity $\vec{V}_{B1}$. The normal direction of the collision, $\hat{N}$, is defined to be the vector between the two circle centers and the tangent direction of the collision, $\hat{T}$, is the vector that is tangential to both of the circles at the point of collision. To resolve this collision, the velocities for shape A and B after the collision, $\vec{V}_{A2}$ and $\vec{V}_{B2}$, must be computed.

The relative velocity between shapes A and B is defined as follows.

- $\vec{V}_{AB1} = \vec{V}_{A1} - \vec{V}_{B1}$

The collision vector decomposition can now be applied to the normal direction of the relative velocity where the relative velocity after the collision is $\vec{V}_{AB2}$.

- $\vec{V}_{AB2} \cdot \hat{N} = -e\left(\vec{V}_{AB1} \cdot \hat{N} \right)$ (1)

The coefficient of restitution, e, models the real-world situation where some kinetic energy is changed to some other form of energy during the collision. Notice that all variables on the right-hand-side of Equation (1) are defined, as they are known at the time of collision, and that the normal component of the relative velocity after the collision of shapes A and B, $\vec{V}_{AB2}$, is also defined. It is important to remember that,

- $\vec{V}_{AB2} = \vec{V}_{A2} - \vec{V}_{B2}$.

You are now ready to approximate $\vec{V}_{A2}$ and $\vec{V}_{B2}$, the velocities of the colliding shapes after the collision.

Approximating the Impulse Response

Accurately describing a collision involves complex considerations including factors like energy changing form, or frictions resulting from different material properties, etc. Without considering these advanced issues, a simplistic description of a collision that occurs on a shape is, a constant mass object changing its velocity from $\vec{V}_{A1}$ to $\vec{V}_{A2}$ after contact with another object. Conveniently, this is the definition of an impulse, as can be seen in the following.

- $j = m_A \vec{V}_{A2} - m_A \vec{V}_{A1}$

Or, when solving for $\vec{V}_{A2}$,

- $\vec{V}_{A2} = \vec{V}_{A1} + \dfrac{j}{m_A}$

Take a step back from the math and think about what this formula states. It makes intuitive sense. It states that the change in velocity is inversely proportional to the mass of a shape. In other words, the more mass a shape has, the less its velocity will change after a collision. The Impulse Method implements this observation, and for the normal component, it defines the velocities after a collision for shapes A and B, $\vec{V}_{A2}$ and $\vec{V}_{B2}$, to be as followed. In this case, m_A and m_B are the masses of Shapes A and B.

- $\vec{V}_{A2} \cdot \hat{N} = \vec{V}_{A1} \cdot \hat{N} + \dfrac{j_N}{m_A}$

- $\vec{V}_{B2} \cdot \hat{N} = \vec{V}_{B1} \cdot \hat{N} - \dfrac{j_N}{m_B}$

Subtracting the above two equations computes the normal component of relative velocity.

- $\left(\vec{V}_{A2} - \vec{V}_{B2} \right) \cdot \hat{N} = \left(\vec{V}_{A1} - \vec{V}_{B1} \right) \cdot \hat{N} + j_N \left(\dfrac{1}{m_A} + \dfrac{1}{m_B} \right)$

Recall that, $\left(\vec{V}_{A2} - \vec{V}_{B2} \right)$ is simply $\vec{V}_{AB2}$, and that, $\left(\vec{V}_{A1} - \vec{V}_{B1} \right)$ is $\vec{V}_{AB1}$, this equation simplifies to the following.

- $\vec{V}_{AB2} \cdot \hat{N} = \vec{V}_{AB1} \cdot \hat{N} + j_N \left(\dfrac{1}{m_A} + \dfrac{1}{m_B} \right)$

Substituting Equation (1) to the left-hand-side and the following equation can be derived.

- $-e \left(\vec{V}_{AB1} \cdot \hat{N} \right) = \vec{V}_{AB1} \cdot \hat{N} + j_N \left(\dfrac{1}{m_A} + \dfrac{1}{m_B} \right)$

Collecting terms, and solving the formula for j_N, the impulse in the normal direction, gives you the following.

- $j_N = \dfrac{-(1+e) \left(\vec{V}_{AB1} \cdot \hat{N} \right)}{\dfrac{1}{m_A} + \dfrac{1}{m_B}}$ (2)

Finally, the impulse in the tangent direction, j_T, can be derived in a similar manner the results of which follow.

$$j_T = \frac{-(1+e)\left(\vec{V}_{AB1} \cdot \hat{T}\right)f}{\dfrac{1}{m_A} + \dfrac{1}{m_B}} \quad (3)$$

The coefficient of friction, f, is a simplistic approximation of friction.

The Steps for Resolving Collisions

You are now ready to modify the resolveCollision function in the Physics.js file to implement the collision resolution between two colliding shapes. The resolution procedure requires access to the two RigidShape objects and the corresponding collision information. The following are the detailed steps involved:

- **Step A**: make sure at least one of the colliding shapes is not static (an inverse mass that is not equal to 0).

- **Step B**: invoke the positional correction function to snap the shapes apart by a percentage of the interpenetration depth. Recall that in your implementation, the colliding shapes will be pushed apart by a default of 80% of the interpenetration depth.

- **Step C**: compute the relative velocity between the two shapes. As presented in the derivation, the relative velocity is essential for computing the impulse in the normal and tangent direction.

- **Step D**: compute the component of the relative velocity that is in the collision normal direction. This component indicates how rapidly the two shapes are moving toward or away from each other. A positive value indicates that the shapes are moving away from each other and impulse response will not be necessary.

- **Step E**: compute the impulse in the normal direction based on results from the previous step, restitution (bounciness), and the masses of the colliding shapes.

- **Step F**: compute the impulse in the tangent direction.

- **Step G**: apply impulses to modify the normal and tangent components of the shapes' velocities to simulate the reflection of both shapes after the collision as well as friction.

The normal and tangent components of the impulse accomplish distinct purposes in simulating the results of a collision. The normal component simulates the bounciness of shapes, while the tangent component handles the friction. As illustrated in Figure 4-7, when a ball is tossed from the left towards the right, its initial spinning direction will determine the motion after the collision with the floor. On the left of Figure 4-7 the ball has an initial counter-clockwise spin while the ball on the right of the figure has an initial clockwise spin. At the point of collision with the floor, the tangent impulse component modified by the respective friction force will either reduce or increase the right-ward linear velocity of the ball depending on its initial spinning direction. This particular functionality will be implemented in the following section on rotational collision response. However, take note that regardless of the objects rotation, upon collision the heights of the balls, after the collision, are equal to each other. This is a result of friction only affecting the tangent impulse component while the restitution affects the normal impulse component.

Figure 4-7. Tangent Component Impulse and Friction

The Collision Impulse Project

This project will guide you through implementing the outlined steps to create a function that resolves the collision between axis-aligned shapes using the Impulse Method. You can see an example of this project running in Figure 4-8. The source code to this project is defined in the Collision Impulse Project folder.

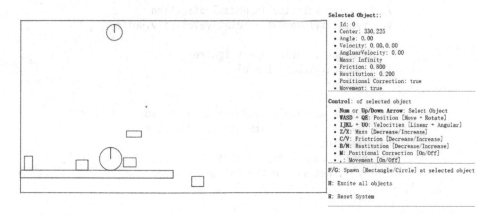

Figure 4-8. Running the Collision Impulse Project

Project Goals:

- To understand the details of Impulse Method computations.

- To build a system that resolves the collision between colliding shapes.

Modify the Physics Engine Component

To properly support collision resolution, you only need to modify the physics.js file to implement the previously outlined steps.

1. Open the Physics.js file and go to the resolveCollision function.

2. After positional correction, you will begin the implementation by computing the collision normal, the relative velocity, the coefficient of restitution and the friction of the colliding shapes.

```
var resolveCollision = function (s1, s2, collisionInfo) {
    if ((s1.mInvMass === 0) && (s2.mInvMass === 0))
        return;

    // correct positions
    if (gEngine.Physics.mPositionalCorrectionFlag)
        positionalCorrection(s1, s2, collisionInfo);

    var n = collisionInfo.getNormal();
    var v1 = s1.mVelocity;
    var v2 = s2.mVelocity;
    var relativeVelocity = v2.subtract(v1);

    // Relative velocity in normal direction
    var rVelocityInNormal = relativeVelocity.dot(n);

    // if objects moving apart ignore
    if (rVelocityInNormal > 0)
        return;

    // compute and apply response impulses for each object
    var newRestituion = Math.min(s1.mRestitution,
    s2.mRestitution);
    var newFriction = Math.min(s1.mFriction, s2.mFriction);
        //... details in the following steps
};
```

3. Compute the impulse in the direction of the collision normal based on Equation (2).

```
//...continue from the previous step
// Calc impulse scalar
var jN = -(1 + newRestituion) * rVelocityInNormal;
jN = jN / (s1.mInvMass + s2.mInvMass);
//... details in the next step
```

4. Apply the impulse to the velocities of the colliding shapes.

```
//...continue from the previous step
//impulse is in direction of normal ( from s1 to s2)
var impulse = n.scale(jN);
// impulse = F dt = m * Δv
// Δv = impulse / m
s1.mVelocity = s1.mVelocity.subtract(impulse.scale(s1.mInvMass));
s2.mVelocity = s2.mVelocity.add(impulse.scale(s2.mInvMass));
//... details in the next step
```

5. Compute the direction that is tangent to the collision normal.

```
//... continue from the previous step
var tangent = relativeVelocity.subtract(
                n.scale(relativeVelocity.dot(n)));
// relativeVelocity.dot(tangent) should less than 0
tangent - tangent.normalize().scale(-1);
//... details in the next step
```

6. Compute the impulse, jT, in the direction that is tangent to
   the collision normal based on Equation (3), and apply the
   impulse to the velocities of the colliding shapes.

```
//...continue from the previous step
var jT = -(1 + newRestituion) *
            relativeVelocity.dot(tangent) * newFriction;
jT = jT / (s1.mInvMass + s2.mInvMass);

// friction should be less than force in normal direction
if (jT > jN) jT = jN;
//impulse is from s1 to s2 (in opposite direction of velocity)
impulse = tangent.scale(jT);

s1.mVelocity = s1.mVelocity.subtract(impulse.scale(s1.mInvMass));
s2.mVelocity = s2.mVelocity.add(impulse.scale(s2.mInvMass));
```

Defining an Initial Rectangle in Mygame.js

You need to modify the Mygame.js file to define an initial rectangular RigidShape object
for testing purposes. Edit Mygame.js and add the following code to define a stationary
rectangle with infinite mass.

```
function MyGame() {
    //...identical to previous project
    var r2 = new Rectangle(new Vec2(200, 400), 400, 20, 0, 1, 0);
    //...identical to previous project
}
```

Observation

You should test your implementation in two ways. First, ensure that moving shapes collide and behave naturally. Second, ensure the collision resolution system is stable when there are many shapes that are in close proximity. You also can test the collision resolution between regular shapes and shapes with infinite mass.

Notice that the scene now has a platform-like shape. This is a shape with infinite mass that can be tested for collision resolution with other regular moving shapes. Now make sure movement is switched on with the comma (,) key and create several rectangle and circle shapes with the F and G keys. Notice that the shapes fall gradually to the floor and their motions stop with a slight rebound. This is a clear indication that the base case for Euler Integration, collision detection, and resolution all are operating as expected. Press the H key to excite all shapes. Notice the wandering shapes interact properly with the platforms and the walls of the game world with soft bounces and no apparent interpenetrations. In addition, pay attention to the apparent transfer of energy during collisions. Try adjusting the shape attributes, for example, the mass, and observe what happens when two shapes with very different masses collide. Notice that the shape with more mass does not change its trajectory much after the collision. Lastly, notice that the shapes do not rotate as a result of collision. That is because your current implementation only considers the linear velocity of the shapes. In the next project you will improve the resolution function to consider angular velocity changes as a result of collisions.

The stability of the system can be tested by increasing the number of shapes in the scene. The relaxation loop count of 15 continuously pushes interpenetrating shapes apart by 80% of the interpenetration depth during each iteration, in addition to the impulse correction. For example, you can switch off movement and positional corrections with the comma and M keys and create multiple, e.g., 10 to 20, overlapping shapes at the exact same position. Now enable position correction with the M key and notice that, after a short pause, the shapes will appear again with no interpenetrations.

Supporting Rotation in Collision Response

Now that you have a concrete understanding and have successfully implemented the Impulse Method for collision responses with linear velocities, it is time to integrate the support for the more general case of rotations. Before discussing the details, it is helpful to relate the relevant correspondences of Newtonian linear mechanics to that of rotational mechanics. That is, linear displacement corresponds to rotation, velocity to angular velocity, force to torque, and mass to rotational inertia. From basic mechanics, rotational inertia is also known as the angular mass. It determines the torque needed for a desired angular acceleration about a rotational axis. The following discussion focuses on integrating rotation into the Impulse Method formulation and does not attempt to present a review on Newtonian Mechanics for Rotation. Conveniently, integrating proper rotation into the Impulse Method does not involve derivation of any new algorithm. All that is required is the formulation of impulse responses with proper consideration of rotational attributes.

Integrating Newtonian Mechanics for Rotation

The key to integrating rotation into the Impulse Method formulation is recognizing the fact that the linear velocity you have been working with, e.g., velocity $\vec{V}_{A1}$ of shape A, is actually the velocity of the shape at its center location. In the absence of rotation, this velocity is constant throughout the shape and can be applied to any position. However, as illustrated in Figure 4-9, when the movement of a shape includes angular velocity, $\vec{\omega}_{A1}$, its linear velocity at a position P, $\vec{V}_{AP1}$, is actually a function of the relative position between the point and the center of rotation of the shape, $\vec{R}_{AP}$.

- $\vec{V}_{AP1} = \vec{V}_{A1} + \left(\vec{\omega}_{A1} \times \vec{R}_{AP} \right)$

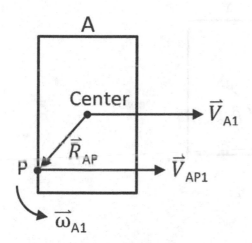

Figure 4-9. *Linear Velocity at a Position in the Presence of Rotation*

■ **Note**   Angular velocity is a vector that is perpendicular to the linear velocity. In this case, as linear velocity is defined on the X/Y plane, $\vec{\omega}$ is a vector in the z direction since objects rotate around their center of mass. For simplicity, in your implementation, $\vec{\omega}$ will be stored as a simple scalar representing the z-component magnitude of the vector.

Formulating Impulse Method with Rotation

Similar to the case for linear impulse response, it is also true that change in angular velocity after a collision is inversely proportional to the rotational inertia. As illustrated in Figure 4-10, for shapes A and B with rotational inertia of I_A and I_B; and initial angular velocities of $\vec{\omega}_{A1}$ and $\vec{\omega}_{B1}$; after a collision the angular velocities, $\vec{\omega}_{A2}$ and $\vec{\omega}_{B2}$, are defined as follows.

- $$\vec{\omega}_{A2} = \vec{\omega}_{A1} + \left(\vec{R}_{AP} \times \hat{N}\right)\frac{j_N}{I_A} + \left(\vec{R}_{AP} \times \hat{T}\right)\frac{j_T}{I_A}$$

- $$\vec{\omega}_{B2} = \vec{\omega}_{B1} + \left(\vec{R}_{BP} \times \hat{N}\right)\frac{j_N}{I_B} + \left(\vec{R}_{BP} \times \hat{T}\right)\frac{j_T}{I_B}$$

Where $\vec{R}_{AP}$ and $\vec{R}_{BP}$ are positional vectors from each shape's center of rotation to the point of collision, P; $\hat{N}$ and $\hat{T}$ are the collision normal and tangent.

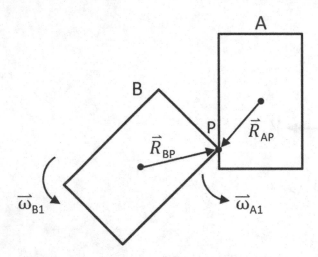

Figure 4-10. *Angular Velocities of two Colliding Shapes*

Recall that the Impulse Method formulation is derived based on decomposing the relative velocity after the collision, $\vec{V}_{AB2} = \vec{V}_{A2} - \vec{V}_{B2}$, into normal and tangent directions. With $\vec{V}_{AB1} = \vec{V}_{A1} - \vec{V}_{B1}$, being the relative velocity from before the collision, Equation (1) from previous section is repeated in the following.

- $$\vec{V}_{AB2} \cdot \hat{N} = -e\left(\vec{V}_{AB1} \cdot \hat{N}\right)$$

Note that this equation was derived before the considerations for rotation and the formulation assumes that the velocity for each shape is constant over the entire shape. In order to support rotation, this equation must be generalized and solved at the point of collision, P.

- $$\vec{V}_{ABP2} \cdot \hat{N} = -e\left(\vec{V}_{ABP1} \cdot \hat{N}\right) \qquad (4)$$

In this case, $\vec{V}_{ABP1}$ and $\vec{V}_{ABP2}$ are relative velocities at collision position P, from before and after the collision where the following is still true for these vectors.

- $\vec{V}_{ABP1} = \vec{V}_{AP1} - \vec{V}_{BP1}$

- $\vec{V}_{ABP2} = \vec{V}_{AP2} - \vec{V}_{BP2}$

As previously derived, it is now possible to substitute the following equations together with the definition of the relative vectors into Equation (4) and solve for the impulse, j.

- $\vec{V}_{AP2} = \vec{V}_{A2} + \left(\vec{\omega}_{A2} \times \vec{R}_{AP} \right)$

- $\vec{V}_{BP2} = \vec{V}_{B2} + \left(\vec{\omega}_{B2} \times \vec{R}_{BP} \right)$

- $\vec{V}_{A2} = \vec{V}_{A1} + \dfrac{j}{m_A}$

- $\vec{V}_{B2} = \vec{V}_{B1} + \dfrac{j}{m_B}$

- $\vec{\omega}_{A2} = \vec{\omega}_{A1} + \left(\vec{R}_{AP} \times \hat{N} \right)\dfrac{j_N}{I_A} + \left(\vec{R}_{AP} \times \hat{T} \right)\dfrac{j_T}{I_A}$

- $\vec{\omega}_{B2} = \vec{\omega}_{B1} + \left(\vec{R}_{BP} \times \hat{N} \right)\dfrac{j_N}{I_B} + \left(\vec{R}_{BP} \times \hat{T} \right)\dfrac{j_T}{I_B}$

Though tedious, the simplification algebra is relatively straightforward, and the resulting impulse in the collision normal direction, j_N, can be expressed as followed.

- $$j_N = \dfrac{-(1+e)\left(\vec{V}_{AB1} \cdot \hat{N} \right)}{\dfrac{1}{m_A} + \dfrac{1}{m_B} + \dfrac{\left(\vec{R}_{AP} \times \hat{N} \right)^2}{I_A} + \dfrac{\left(\vec{R}_{BP} \times \hat{N} \right)^2}{I_B}} \qquad (5)$$

Similar to the case in linear response, the impulse in the tangent direction, j_T, can be derived and expressed as followed.

- $$j_T = \dfrac{-(1+e)\left(\vec{V}_{AB1} \cdot \hat{T} \right)f}{\dfrac{1}{m_A} + \dfrac{1}{m_B} + \dfrac{\left(\vec{R}_{AP} \times \hat{T} \right)^2}{I_A} + \dfrac{\left(\vec{R}_{BP} \times \hat{T} \right)^2}{I_B}} \qquad (6)$$

Once again, the coefficient of friction, f, is a simplistic approximation of friction. In addition, note that since $\vec{R}_{AP}$ and $\hat{N}$ are vectors in the X/Y plane, in implementation $\vec{R}_{AP} \times \hat{N}$ is a scalar representing the z-component magnitude of the resulting vector.

You are now ready to implement Impulse Method collision response with support for rotation, or angular impulse.

The Angular Impulse Project

This project will guide you through the implementation of angular impulse. You can see an example of this project running in Figure 4-11. The source code to this project is defined in the Angular Impulse Project folder.

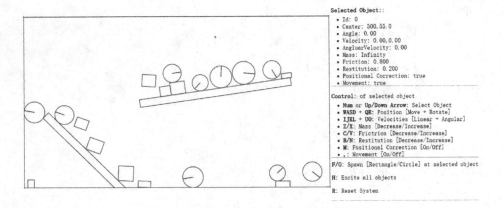

***Figure 4-11.** Running the Angular Impulse Project*

Project Goals:

- To understand the details of angular impulse

- To integrate rotation into your collision resolution

- To complete the physics component

To implement angular impulse, in the resolve collision function, you only need to modify the Physics.js file to implement the generalized formulation derived.

1. Edit the Physics.js file and go to resolveCollision function that you have created in the previous projects.

2. It is important to compute the velocities at the collision position, $\vec{V}_{AP1}$ and $\vec{V}_{BP1}$. In the following, r1 and r2 are the $\vec{R}_{AP}$ and $\vec{R}_{AP}$ positional vectors for shapes A and B. Notice that in the implementation, the collision position, P, is simply the mStart position in the collisionInfo. The variables v1 and v2 are the actual $\vec{V}_{AP1}$ and $\vec{V}_{BP1}$ vectors.

```
var resolveCollision = function (s1, s2, collisionInfo) {
    //..identical to previous project
    var n = collisionInfo.getNormal();
    //the direction of collisionInfo is always from s1 to s2
    //but the Mass is inversed, so start scale with s2 and end
    scale with s1
    var start = collisionInfo.mStart.scale(s2.mInvMass /
    (s1.mInvMass + s2.mInvMass));
    var end = collisionInfo.mEnd.scale(s1.mInvMass /
    (s1.mInvMass + s2.mInvMass));
    var p = start.add(end);
    //r is vector from center of shape to collision point
    var r1 = p.subtract(s1.mCenter);
    var r2 = p.subtract(s2.mCenter);

    //newV = V + mAngularVelocity cross R
    var v1 = s1.mVelocity.add(new Vec2(-1 * s1.mAngularVelocity * r1.y,
                                       s1.mAngularVelocity * r1.x));
    var v2 = s2.mVelocity.add(new Vec2(-1 * s2.mAngularVelocity * r2.y,
                                       s2.mAngularVelocity * r2.x));
    var relativeVelocity = v2.subtract(v1);

    // Relative velocity in normal direction
    var rVelocityInNormal = relativeVelocity.dot(n);

    //..details in the next step
};
```

3. The next step is to compute the impulse in the collision
    normal direction, j_N, according to Equation (5).

```
//...identical to previous project
//...continue from previous step
var newFriction = Math.min(s1.mFriction, s2.mFriction);
//R cross N
var R1crossN = r1.cross(n);
var R2crossN = r2.cross(n);

// Calc impulse scalar
// Reference: http://www.myphysicslab.com/collision.html
var jN = -(1 + newRestituion) * rVelocityInNormal;
jN = jN / (s1.mInvMass + s2.mInvMass +
        R1crossN * R1crossN * s1.mInertia +
        R2crossN * R2crossN * s2.mInertia);
//...details in the next step
```

4. Now, update the angular velocity according to the Impulse Method formulation introduced.

```
s1.mAngularVelocity -= R1crossN * jN * s1.mInertia;
s2.mAngularVelocity += R2crossN * jN * s2.mInertia;
//...details in the next step
```

5. Now, compute the impulse in the collision tangent direction, j_T, according to Equation (6).

```
//...identical to previous project
//relativeVelocity.dot(tangent) should less than 0
tangent = tangent.normalize().scale(-1);

var R1crossT = r1.cross(tangent);
var R2crossT = r2.cross(tangent);

var jT = -(1 + newRestituion) *
        relativeVelocity.dot(tangent) *
        newFriction;
jT = jT / (s1.mInvMass + s2.mInvMass +
        R1crossT * R1crossT * s1.mInertia +
        R2crossT * R2crossT * s2.mInertia);
//...identical to previous project
```

6. Finally, update the angular velocity based on the tangent direction impulse

```
s1.mAngularVelocity -= R1crossT * jT * s1.mInertia;
s2.mAngularVelocity += R2crossT * jT * s2.mInertia;
```

Observation

Run the project to test your implementation. The shape that you insert into the scene should now be rotating, colliding, and responding in fashions that are similar to the real world. A circle shape rolls around when other shapes collide with them, while a rectangle shape should rotate naturally upon collision. The interpenetration between shapes should not be visible under normal circumstances. However, two reasons can still cause observable interpenetrations. First, a small relaxation iteration, or second, your CPU is struggling with the number of shapes. In the first case, you can try increasing the relaxation iteration to prevent any interpenetration. Now your 2D physics engine implementation is completed. You can continue testing by creating additional shapes to observe when your CPU begins to struggle with keep up real time performance.

Summary

This chapter has guided you through understanding the foundation behind a working physics engine. A step-by-step derivation of the relevant formulae for the simulations followed by a detailed guide to the building of a functioning system. You have computed the movement of shapes, resolved interpenetrations after collisions, implemented resolution based on the Impulse Method for shapes both linearly and rotationally. Now that you have completed your physics engine, you can integrate the system into almost any 2D game engine. Additionally, you can test your implementation by supporting other shapes. You can also carefully examine the system and identify potentials for optimization and further abstractions. Many improvements to the physics engine are still possible.

CHAPTER 5

■ ■ ■

Summarizing the Physics Engine

Congratulations! You have learned the basic ideas and concepts behind and completed the implementation of a 2D physics engine. This chapter will summarize all of your work done from Chapter 1 to 4, what you should understand and take away from this book, and highlight improvements or future explorations on the physics engine that you have created.

This chapter begins by summarizing all of the physics engine theories and concepts that you have learned and used throughout the book. Next, a detailed list of source code files, and the associated functions that you have written are presented, serving as a simple "readme" file. Lastly, further topics you can explore and possibly implement in your physics engine will be presented as a starting point for your future endeavors with game physics engines. This chapter will also include a simple project serving as the final and complete functionality and features testing of your engine. You can follow the project guide on setting up and running the simulation, or be creative and set up your own test cases.

The Concepts and Theories

This book is designed to guide you to build your own physics simulation. As such, all topics introduced relate to the building of such a system.

- **Rigid Shape** - A primitive that does not change its shape during physical interaction. In order to support efficient interaction simulation, these are usually simple geometric shapes, e.g., circles and rectangles. A rigid shape has its own attributes that support physics simulation such as mass, width, height, center of gravity, inertia, friction, restitution, etc.

- **Engine Loop** - A continuous running loop that updates the object states, invokes the calculations of inter-object interactions, and renders the objects. The engine loop must cycle through all operations and maintain a real-time performance. By implementing a fixed time step update in the loop, it becomes straightforward to simulate movement integration and maintain a deterministic game state.

© Michael Tanaya, Huaming Chen, Jebediah Pavleas and Kelvin Sung 2017
M. Tanaya et al., *Building a 2D Game Physics Engine*, DOI 10.1007/978-1-4842-2583-7_5

- **Collision Detection** - An algorithm to determine if objects have overlapped and/or interpenetrated other objects.

- **Broad Phase Method** - An optimization for collision detection by exploiting the proximity of objects. Axis-aligned bounding boxes are used by the engine to reduce the overhead of invoking actual collision detection algorithms.

- **Separating Axis Theorem** - One of the most popular algorithms for detecting collisions between general convex shapes in 2D. It is typically preceded with an initial pass of a broad phase method to improve its overall performance. This algorithm can detect collisions between axis-aligned as well as rotated shapes.

- **Collision Information** - The information describing the details of a collision including interpenetration depth, normal direction that caused the interpenetration, and beginning and end of an interpenetration. This information is essential for resolving a collision.

- **Symplectic Euler Integration** - A method of approximating integrals based on initial values. This engine uses the Symplectic Euler Integration to approximate an object's new linear and rotational velocities, and its new position.

- **Positional Correction** - The process of separating two interpenetration objects using collision information collected during collision detection.

- **Relaxation Loop** - An iterative loop in the core of the physics engine that repeatedly and incrementally apply positional correction on interpenetrating objects in an attempt to remove the occurrence of colliding object interpenetration.

- **Impulse Method** - A largely simplified, physically-based collision response formulation that is capable of capturing object bounciness and friction considerations during a collision.

- **Collision Resolution** - A process that determines how objects should respond after a collision. When applying the Impulse Method to resolve a collision, colliding objects receive new linear and angular velocities.

The Engine Source Code

The following is the list of source code files and the associated functionality.

- `Core.js`
  - Core engine loop
  - Update function

- Drawing function
- UI control

- Physics.js
  - Collision detection
  - Relaxation loop
  - Positional correction
  - Resolving collision

- CollisionInfo.js
  - Collision information object
  - Constructor and getter/setter

- Vec2.js
  - 2D vector calculation

- RigidShape.js
  - Base class of rigid shape
  - Constructor
  - Update function
  - Bounding box collision test for broad phase method support

- Rectangle.js & Circle.js
  - Inherit from rigid shape base class
  - Specific constructor for each
  - Rotate function
  - Draw function
  - Move function

- Rectangle_collision.js & Circle_collision.js
  - Collision detection functions
  - Gather collision information

- UserControl.js
  - User input controller

- `MyGame.js`
  - Simulation scene controller
- `Index.html`
  - Script calling
  - Initialize simulation scene

The Cool Demo Project

This project guides you in setting up the scene to test the functionality of your physics engine implementation. You can see an example of this project running in Figure 5-1. The source code to this project is defined in the A Cool Demo Project folder.

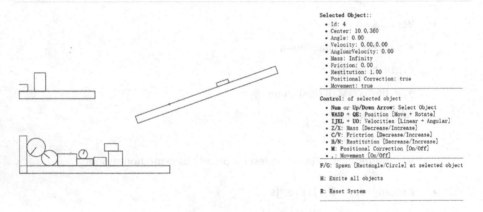

Figure 5-1. *Running the Cool Demo Project*

Project Goal:

- To test and engage with all the functionalities and features of the physics engine

Modifying Simulation Scene

Let's start by modifying the simulation scene:

1. Edit the `MyGame.js` file.

2. Replace all the code inside the `MyGame` constructor to create a new scene for the simulation.

```
"use strict";
/* global height, width, gEngine */
function MyGame() {
}
```

3. In the MyGame constructor, create four platforms, with one
   rotated for testing the angular movements.

```
//...continue from previous step
var r1 = new Rectangle(new Vec2(500, 200), 400, 20, 0, 0.3, 0);
r1.rotate(2.8);
var r2 = new Rectangle(new Vec2(200, 400), 400, 20, 0, 1, 0.5);
var r3 = new Rectangle(new Vec2(100, 200), 200, 20, 0);
var r4 = new Rectangle(new Vec2(10, 360), 20, 100, 0, 0, 1);
//...more in next step
```

4. Create 10 circle and rectangle objects with random attributes
   to begin with the simulation.

```
//...continue from previous step
for (var i = 0; i < 10; i++) {
  var r1 = new Rectangle(
              new Vec2(Math.random() * gEngine.Core.mWidth,
                   Math.random() * gEngine.Core.mHeight / 2),
              Math.random() * 50 + 10, Math.random() * 50 + 10,
              Math.random() * 30, Math.random(), Math.random());
    r1.mVelocity = new Vec2(Math.random() * 60 - 30,
                       Math.random() * 60 - 30);
    r1 = new Circle(
            new Vec2(Math.random() * gEngine.Core.mWidth,
               Math.random() * gEngine.Core.mHeight / 2),
            Math.random() * 20 + 10, Math.random() * 30,
            Math.random(), Math.random());
    r1.mVelocity = new Vec2(Math.random() * 60 - 30,
                       Math.random() * 60 - 30);
}
```

Observation

You can see that there are no borders in the scene. This allows objects to fall off the screen
and not crowd the space. In this way you can continue to create new objects and observe
the simulation of object behaviors. You can also test the performance of your engine by
creating more objects at the beginning of the simulation. Note that this book provides
you with the basic understanding of creating your own physics engine. There is plenty
of room for improvements, ranging from choosing alternative algorithms, supporting
different features, to optimizing the efficiency of the calculations, etc. The next section
will point out some of the topics you could look into to improve your engine.

Further Exploration and Related Topics

With your physics engine now completed you may be asking yourself, what now? How should I proceed with the knowledge I have gained, what should I do with the physics engine I created or what should I learn next? Ultimately, as is most often the case, the answer is that it depends. It depends on your interests in game physics engines in the first place and why you decided to read and follow along with this book. If your desire was to create a game or game engine from scratch, you may wish to integrate this physics engine into your own game engine or an existing game engine in order to add rigid body physics functionality to the project. If your reason had a more academic nature with the goal of learning and understanding how game physics engines function you may want to explore further into related topics within game physics.

Regardless of which category you lie in, you may wish to extend the functionality of the physics engine by improving its performance and capabilities by adding more advanced features or components. If that is the case, then the following topics provide you with some suggested jumping off points for further exploration within game physics.

Physics Topics

- **Advanced 2-D Rigid Body Physics** - If you enjoyed the Impulse Method approach and are looking to improve the functionality of your physics engine by adding features such as kinematics (often used for moving platforms), joints (for more complex rigid body behavior), or a host of other great features, we suggest that you look at the Box2D physics engine and the literature from its creator, Erin Catto. Box2D is the game physics engine that popularized the Impulse Method and is available in several programming languages.

  http://box2d.org/

- **Verlet Physics** - If you're looking to simulate soft body physics, then we suggest exploring Verlet physics. Verlet physics provides a fast and simple way to simulate soft bodies, such as rag dolls, ropes, jelly-like objects and even cloth, through the use of particles, constraints (springs) and Verlet Integration to build complex soft-bodied objects. In particular, we suggest you take a look at Thomas Jakobsen's paper on *Advanced Character Physics*, which is probably the most popular starting point for people interested in game physics, due to its ease of implementation and understandability. The downside of Verlet physics is the potential of instability when applied to rigid body simulations.

- **Networked Physics** - The subject of networked physics contains its own unique set of problems that need to be addressed, many of which revolve around synchronization. To get your bearings on the subject, we suggest you take a look at the following website.

http://gafferongames.com/game-physics/

- **3-D Rigid Body Physics** - If you're interested in venturing into 3-D physics simulations, a great starting point is the Impulse Method! The great thing about the Impulse Method is that it can also be used in 3-D physics, as well as 2-D. Newcastle University provides some great information on implementing the impulse method in 3-D.

  https://research.ncl.ac.uk/game/mastersdegree/gametechnologies/

Collision Detection Topics

- **Continuous Collision** - Continuous collision is a method to solve the problem of physics objects passing through other physics object geometries that are too small or traveling at too high velocities. This is a problem due to the discrete time step nature of game engines. There are several approaches to address this problem. A great place to start and get your bearings for the topic is Erin Catto's GDC (Game Developers Conference) presentation.

  http://www.gdcvault.com/play/1018239/Physics-for-Game-Programmers Continuous

- **Collision Callbacks** - Collision callbacks provide a more advanced and flexible collision behavior. They can be used to customize the behavior for your physics objects such as OnCollisionEnter or OnCollisionExit. In addition, they can also be useful for passing any collision information needed for any game logic. Collision callbacks are often a key feature for more advanced physics engines.

- **GJK Collision Detection** - The GJK (Gilbert-Johnson-Keerthi) algorithm is an alternate collision detection method to the Separating Axis Theorem. GJK provides more flexibility and performs collision detection for many-sided convex polygons.

- **Spatial Partitioning** - Spatial partitioning is a more advanced broad phase method commonly used in physics engines to improve performance for both collision detection and response. The method divides the world space into discrete areas in order to detect likely collisions. One of the more commonly used spatial partitioning techniques in 2D is known as quad-tree.

Reference

The following are some of the references we consulted when we learned this topic.

- General definitions: https://en.wikipedia.org/

- Physic shape and attributes: http://buildnewgames.com/gamephysics/

- Separating Axis Theorem: http://www.metanetsoftware.com/technique/tutorialA.html#section3

- Resolve collision without rotation: https://gamedevelopment.tutsplus.com/tutorials/how-to-create-a-custom-2d-physics-engine-friction-scene-and-jump-table--gamedev-7756

- The formula of impulse in collision with rotation: http://www.myphysicslab.com/collision.html

- Resolve collision rotation and Separating Axis Theorem: https://gamedevelopment.tutsplus.com/tutorials/how-to-create-a-custom-2d-physics-engine-oriented-rigid-bodies--gamedev-8032

Index

© Michael Tanaya, Huaming Chen, Jebediah Pavleas and Kelvin Sung 2017
M. Tanaya et al., *Building a 2D Game Physics Engine*, DOI 10.1007/978-1-4842-2583-7

Get the eBook for only $4.99!

Why limit yourself?

Now you can take the weightless companion with you wherever you go and access your content on your PC, phone, tablet, or reader.

Since you've purchased this print book, we are happy to offer you the eBook for just $4.99.

Convenient and fully searchable, the PDF version enables you to easily find and copy code—or perform examples by quickly toggling between instructions and applications.

To learn more, go to http://www.apress.com/us/shop/companion or contact support@apress.com

Printed in the United States
By Bookmasters